ACTIVATING YOUR GOD-GIVEN POWER TO CREATE REALMS AND ATMOSPHERES

CREATE YOUR WORLD

Create Your World!

Activating your God-given power
to create realms and atmospheres

Patricia King

BONUS BOOK: God Loves You With An Everlasting Love

Published by XP Publishing
P. O. Box 1017
Maricopa, Arizona 85139
XPpublishing.com

ISBN: 978-1-936101-77-1

ENDORSEMENTS

From Kris Vallotton:

Jesus promised us an "abundant life" full of adventure. Yet many believers live such a boring existence that their lives are sort of a cosmic yawn rather than an inspiring exploit that employs angelic reinforcements. Novels, movies, the Internet, television, and talk shows syphon off their desire for passionate pursuits. Consequently, they spend most of their existence waiting for life to begin. Patricia King's book, *Create Your World*, reawakens the divine passions of "the people who know their God [to] be strong, and carry out *great exploits*" (Daniel 11:32 NKJV), that they may embrace their God-given purpose.

Patricia is a radical Christian whose very life is an inspiration. Her book reads like a warrior's journal written by one of King David's mighty men. *Create Your World* will challenge, inspire, equip, and thrust you onto the fast track to *your* great adventure. I dare you to read this book!

KRIS VALLOTTON
Senior Associate Leader of Bethel Church, Redding, CA
Co-Founder of Bethel School of Supernatural Ministry
Author of eight books, including *The Supernatural Ways of Royalty and Spirit Wars*

From Matt Sorger:

Patricia King has written a book that will empower you to frame your world and experience the kind of life Jesus died to give you. *Create Your World* is full of keys that will help you unlock your full potential and transform every aspect of your life. By understanding the power of your choices, thoughts, associations, and so much more, you can see God's fullest and richest blessings released. Get ready to overcome a life of defeat and mediocrity and excel into the success and favor you were destined to have. As you read and apply the principles of *Create Your World,* your relationships, health, finances, and overall state of being will be supernaturally blessed by God! This book is a must read for those who want to live in maximum blessing.

MATT SORGER
President of Matt Sorger Ministries
Host of TV's Power for Life

From Dr. Clarice Fluitt:

Patricia King has a gift of skillfully reducing profound knowledge to a level of comprehension that helps ordinary people to understand extraordinary truth.

Jesus was an amazing storyteller and so is Patricia King. This book, *Create Your World,* will stir the reader's faith to ratify, activate, and prophesy the infallible Word of God over their lives. This is a "now" book that does not talk about *someday* God will or *yesterday* God did, but *today* He is doing. It has a razor-sharp edge that separates the soul from the spirit, the Adamic nature from the Christ nature, and sounds a prophetic trumpet to the redeemed to come into agreement with God!

When God called Abraham, he moved in obedience by faith, and God promised that through him all the nations of the earth would be blessed. Abraham's faith in God and his influence changed the atmosphere of everyone he encountered. Through Abraham's legacy, Jesus Christ, the Word of God, came to save humanity and provide mankind a personal relationship with God and eternal blessing.

Consider the pattern of this amazing story. God called Patricia King, she moved by faith, and the nations of the earth are blessed. Patricia's faith in God influences the atmosphere of all who come in contact with her. Through her spiritual lineage, Jesus Christ is born again into hungry hearts. This is "God's way," and He wants to use this same pattern with you – to change *your* world and even the entire earth.

Dr. Clarice Fluitt
President and Founder of Clarice Fluitt Ministries
Co-Founder/Co-Pastor of Eagles Nest World Prayer & Training Ctr.
CEO of The Gennao Group Int'l, Transformational Leadership Coach

From James Goll:

You are holding in your hand a "stick of dynamite" that, when read and applied, will blow away doubt, unbelief, and any other obstacle or hindrance standing between your destiny revealed and destiny fulfilled. In Christ Jesus, you can shift atmospheres and create realms where "all things are possible." In each generation, God raises up pioneers who forge a way so the rest of the body of Christ can benefit from their remarkable breakthroughs. My friend, Patricia King, keeps taking more territory for Jesus' sake!

Dr. James W. Goll
President of Encounters Network
Director of Prayer Storm

From Joan Hunter:

As Sons of God, we have the freedom, authority, and power to create the world we want around us. In Patricia King's new book, *Create Your World*, she gives clear and simple guidelines so every believer can live a life of victory rather than as a victim, an overcomer rather than a life of defeat. If (when) you put into practice the principles in this book, you will walk in an atmosphere of blessing, down a road of peace, to a place of fullness and glory, regardless of what is going on in the world around you!

JOAN HUNTER
Author/Evangelist

From Mark Chironna:

Don't be hasty as you read this marvelous book – it is a treasure trove of Kingdom keys and insights into the creative power Christ has placed in you. If you heed what Patricia shares, allow her to guide you step by step, and reach out your hand to take the keys she extends, you will unlock doors that hold untold possibilities and promises that will enable you to *Create Your World*.

MARK J. CHIRONNA, MA, PHD
Mark Chironna Ministries

From Iverna Tompkins:

Feeling powerless and confused in these troubled times? Want to know a way out? Here is a book that gives both practical and spiritual direction for us to be able to create our own world.

In these bewildering days, with so many voices seeking our attention, we need to know the truth that sets us free – free to be and do all our Creator has empowered us for. Please do not reject this book because you have heard some teaching (that had no biblical balance) promising that whatever you name and claim, you possess. Maybe you even tried it yourself, but it didn't work.

Now you think even the suggestion that Christians can "create" seems somewhat heretical. If so, you are the very person who will be set free from confusion as you read *Create Your World*.

I encourage you to read it all the way through with an open heart, and you will find an open heaven of blessing over your life, home, and business. I like this book. I'm glad I read this book and I plan to share it with others.

DR. IVERNA TOMPKINS
Iverna Tompkins Ministries

From Keith Miller:

As I read *Create Your World,* I was stirred immediately. This book will enrich all who read it. Patricia unfolds, and brings understanding to, the power in our ability to speak and be in agreement with the heart of the Lord, who establishes, forms, and changes the atmospheres around us for our lives, families, communities, and nation. I would recommend this book to be one of those "must reads." Patricia isn't just writing a book. She's sharing out of her own walk and spiritual understanding to impact your everyday life. This book will be an eye-opener for you to walk in greater levels of breakthrough.

KEITH MILLER
Stand Firm World Ministries

From Faytene Grasseschi:

If there is anyone who has the authority to speak on this topic, it is Patricia King. I have seen her create her world and impact the worlds of others through the principles found in this book. Really, this is a perfect read for anyone who is wanting to reach their God-given potential in a life for Christ.

FAYTENE GRASSESCHI
Preacher, Author, Activist

From Dr. Ché Ahn:

In a world facing transition and upheaval, it is vital that believers in Christ understand their power to call forth light into darkness and order into chaos. I highly recommend Patricia King's book, *Create Your World*, where she shows you how to operate in your God-given authority to bring heaven to earth and create environments of love, hope, victory, and faith in every facet of life.

Dr. Ché Ahn
Senior Pastor, HROCK Church, Pasadena, CA
President, Harvest International Ministry

From Joshua & Janet Angela Mills:

Patricia King's book, *Create Your World*, is an invitation to explore, discover, and begin to change the atmosphere in your life. Within its pages you will find helpful keys and practical suggestions for connecting with the abundant blessings of God. You will especially enjoy reading Patricia's real-life testimonies of changing realms and atmospheres. We think you will enjoy this book as much as we did!

Joshua & Janet Angela Mills
Evangelists, New Wine International, Inc.
Palm Springs, CA/Vancouver, BC
www.NewWineInternational.org

CONTENTS

Create Your World

Bonus Book:

God Loves You... With an Everlasting Love

ACKNOWLEDGEMENTS

Thank you to all our team at XPministries. I am so thankful to work with such a group of faithful, committed believers.

A special thanks to Carol Martinez with XP Publishing and Larry Witten, my editor on this project.

Thank you to my husband Ron who is such a constant, living example to me of unconditional love, patience, and encouragement.

Thank you to all my wonderful mentors in the faith who over the years taught me to always believe the Word and the promises of God.

And above all:

Thank You Holy Spirit — my Mentor and Friend!

FOREWORD

Mark Chironna

Take the Keys to Unlock Your World

It has been said that "words create worlds." Indeed this is true, given the fact that the entire universe displays the signature of God, and He literally spoke the universe into existence.

The very first revelation of God in Scripture is of God the Creator. By ten decrees of "let there be" over six days, He created three realms the first three days, and during the second three-day period, He populated those realms by the spoken, creative, "proceeding word."

After the first seven "let there be" decrees, God's eighth proclamation took creation to an entirely new level. The Creator declared, "Let Us make man in Our image and likeness." Then the Godhead took the least valuable substance on earth – dust – and with pure artistry fashioned mankind. Male and female, He created them in His image and likeness, and gave them rulership over all His handiwork.

Being made in the image of God indicates that at the core of our humanness, we are creators. Indeed, we were called to express our "creative DNA" in every aspect and sphere of life. All too often, people dismiss the reality of *being creative*, because they equate creativity to a small segment of the human population. Erroneously, they believe that creativity is only useful to those who fashion things of beauty recognized as "works of art."

How sad that so many people diminish their own creative capabilities and thereby fail to experience their full potential. They disqualify themselves merely because they do not believe they are creative. The truth is, you cannot be a human being, made in the "Imago Dei," and not be creative. The fact is, you are far more creative than you realize, and in more ways than you might think.

In the Kingdom of God, access to the flow of God's creative power requires opening the doorway to its release. The hinges of that doorway are twofold: *words spoken* with conviction and authority, empowered by the indwelling Spirit of God; and *deeds done* with assurance, conviction, and intention by the inspiration of God's Spirit.

The activation of these two dimensions – the work of your words and the work of your hands – reveal that you are a child of God. In making you, God first worked with His words and then with His hands. When the Artist stepped back to view His finished work, His evaluation and judgment of man was, "It is very good!"

Through sin, humanity fell into a place of alienation from God, from themselves, and from each other. Consequently, it took another Man, who is the express image and likeness of God, to deal with the sin issue and restore us to our place of absolute potential and creativity through Himself. Now, Christ IN YOU enables you to operate in the highest level of creative power. He who created the world wants to create again in *you*, with *you*, and through *you*!

Much of the interior landscape of your regenerated spirit and renewed soul has yet to be explored. Hidden within your inner being are latent potentialities and possibilities, gifts and capacities for creating your world. In fact, within you lies the ability to create a world others will want to belong to.

This is your opportune time to explore the landscape of your creative being and find the signature of the Artist within. Your journey toward self-awareness and self-discovery awaits only your willingness to activate it by faith. Doors to that rich inner world will spring open when you decide you are ready to walk through them.

The truth is – when you allow all your inner doors to be opened, those outer doors, to things that you never dreamed possible, will also open automatically. Creation must bow to your right as a child of God to set it free from the futility to which it has been subjected since the fall of man.

You are part of God's restoration program to "heaven-ize" the earth with the glory He has placed in you, so the whole earth can be filled with His glory.

By the way, the ONLY atmosphere God moves in ... creates in ... and speaks in is His GLORY! And since you are made in His image, GLORY is the only realm where your creativity can achieve its full potential.

The really great news is that right now you hold in your hands a set of God-designed keys that lead to twelve doors, and when you use those keys to unlock those doors, creativity will pour out of your being. Patricia King has charted a course for you to explore every one of the twelve dimensions that lead to living a creative life. They enable you to *create your world* from the inside out, by the power of the indwelling Spirit of God.

Patricia King is a pioneer leading the charge into greater expressions of God's creative touch in the lives of His sons and daughters. She has plowed ground that others only dreamed of, and she has skillfully fleshed out a series of pathways for the children of God to find their creative niche. She is well qualified to take you on this creative journey because she is living it, and God continues to bless and enlarge her spheres as she persists in honing and sharpening her creative skills in His Spirit.

Don't be hasty as you read this marvelous book; it is a treasure trove of Kingdom keys and insights into the creative power Christ has placed in you. If you heed what Patricia shares, allow her to guide you step by step, and reach out your hand to take the keys she extends, you will unlock doors that hold untold possibilities and promises that will enable you to *Create Your World*.

MARK J. CHIRONNA, MA, PHD
Mark Chironna Ministries
Orlando, Florida

FOREWORD

Graham Cooke

The issue of "realms" and "atmosphere" is what separates a New Testament disciple from the old covenant believer. Before the Christ era, people lived in a *visitation culture*. Their atmosphere was the altar, the tabernacle, and the temple. Each was an external place God's people visited to further and upgrade their involvement with God.

In the new covenant we have a *habitation culture*, because God makes His home within us. Our hearts become His dwelling place and we explore the delights of "abiding in Christ," an entirely different *realm* for an entirely new creation. In Christ all the old realms have passed away. The new realms have come and taken the presence of God from the temple without to the temple within. We are a spiritual realm because God is in us – Christ in us the expectation of glory. A realm has settled into our hearts that empowers us to live from a dynamic, internal perspective.

Jesus within creates a new atmosphere that upgrades our earthly personality to a heavenly persona (identity, personality, and role). We are seated above in heavenly places, and through this dynamic placement, we can receive a new *realm of authority*. We are citizens of heaven residing on earth – a truth that provokes us into a new perspective; a better way of thinking with a fresh language of the

Spirit to express its reality. Where Jesus is (in relation to everyone and everything), there we may be also.

This new realm of identity and relationship takes us from being overcomers to becoming "more than conquerors."

An overcomer is one who has battled through, persisted and, as a result, has tasted victory. A person becomes "more than a conqueror" when their *internal atmosphere* is so strong that the enemy fails to show up for the fight or flees the battlefield. This new realm dictates that all things *will* work together for good because all things are in subjection under the feet of Jesus. All things become possible as doubt, fear, anxiety, and unbelief are expelled from the realm we occupy.

Identity is the key to transformation. We behave according to how we see ourselves (positive or negative). In this new realm of Christ within, we choose the identity that expresses God's principle desire for us, which becomes our inner atmosphere. We maintain that inner atmosphere by remaining true to God's view of us. Abiding in Christ creates the realm that allows us to come before the Father in the same manner that Jesus would Himself.

In this new realm, we choose our identity before we face the issue. This allows us to create a clearing in the woods, so to speak, to take a deep breath, relax, be at peace, and hear what the Spirit is saying. We partner with the Holy Spirit to create, establish, and maintain our inner realm. I love the Holy Spirit. I love how He adores Jesus. I especially love the enthusiasm He has to make us in God's image.

A realm, an inner atmosphere, provides us with a focus that empowers our favor to rise up to the level of the relationship that is shared between the Son and the Father.

I know Patricia well. When she speaks or writes, it is with an engaging passion for the word that God has laid upon her heart. This book is typical Patricia. Well thought through, passionately prayed into being, and each chapter dripping with intention. This book will take your heart in the direction it is longing to go. It will create a living picture of the territory where you can learn to live, move, and have your very being. It offers lots of practical steps in how to get there and powerful insights to empower your journey.

GRAHAM COOKE
www.brilliantbookhouse.com

1

THE GATE TO GOODNESS

1

The Gate to Goodness

*No one deliberately chooses
a life of failure and despair,
A humdrum life going nowhere,
So why do so many people live there?*

Everyone would choose a life filled with blessing and success, yet many do not experience it. Therefore, the all-important question is: Why do people who believe that God gives the power to create a blessed life live below their potential, and how can they find their way to the blessing realm? The answer to that question requires a book ... this is that book.

I have observed three types of people in the world; perhaps you have noticed them, too.

First, there is the person who appears to succeed at everything. It is as though a realm of favor, joy, pleasure, and success surrounds them and influences every aspect of their life. Their relationships, career, health, and material possessions all appear to pulsate with goodness and fruitfulness.

On the other hand, you have probably met individuals in the second category who live with constant patterns of failure.

They exist in a realm of continual disappointments, tragedies, broken dreams, and shattered hopes.

The third group includes those who live their lives somewhere in-between the first type and the second – sometimes things work out well for them and sometimes they don't. Their lives seem to contain a little bit of blessing and a little bit of curse, with a whole lot of mediocrity in between. Some think this is the "normal life."

This may sound like a dumb question, but you must answer it to experience change:

If you became convinced that you actually possess the God-given authority to create a life of blessing and success, would you be willing to pay the price – give up old ways of thinking, speaking, and acting – to learn new ways that are required for greater success in life?

The Bible is your handbook for living the optimal life. It contains all the wisdom, insights, and counsel you need to live a life of abundance, purity, and fruitfulness. In the Word, you find the keys to transform yourself and the world you influence. The Word of God works for all people, even those who are unaware they are obeying it. It is the same with the natural laws created by God … the law of gravity works whether you are a Christian or not. The principles and instruction we discover in God's Word will create results for all who obey and align with it.

You *CAN* Create Your World!

I am confident that if you really believed you had the power to create your world, you would wholeheartedly fashion an environment of "heaven on earth" in every area. It would be a world full of love, joy, peace, and all that gives you pleasure.

The truth is, you actually do have a God-given ability to create your life, and you can greatly influence all that pertains to you. The first step toward taking control of your world is understanding and accepting that, for the most part, you have created the current state of your life. You probably did not try to, or even realize that you were creating "your world" by your attitudes, choices, and actions, but you were ... and you still are.

> You actually do have a God-given ability to create your life, and you can greatly influence all that pertains to you.

Obstacles or Opportunities

I once met a woman living in a devastating situation. Through no fault of her own her marriage had failed; her husband left her for another man (yes, another *man*). In addition, she experienced bankruptcy and had serious health issues. When I suggested that she had the power to create a life full of blessing, freedom, and health rather than live under the heavy weights she was carrying, she became defensive and somewhat angry with me.

She argued that her life was the result of the decisions of others – choices she had no power over. She further stated that these "things" had caused her hellish existence and she did not believe it could ever be different. I explained that I did not intend to be condemning or accusatory but was attempting to bring hope and inspire faith. I pointed out that the outcome of her life was in *her* hands because **in Christ, she was a victor, not a victim.** I further explained that *if* she chose to abide in the peace of Christ during this devastating time and made use of her God-given power to *create her world*, she could experience wholeness and a glorious future. She could choose to create a great life for the rest of her days or live a depressing life of bondage, remorse, and bitterness.

I shared that in Christ and through Him, she had the power to rule and reign over her present and future, and by posturing herself in faith she could expect goodness to be returned on every wave. Her husband's failures did not have to cause *her failure*. Her painful situation could be either an obstacle or an opportunity – it was actually *her* choice. She could even make the devil sorry that he had ever attacked her by creating an amazing future for herself and her two young children. What is the popular saying? "Success is the best revenge."

All she could *see* was the mess her husband's actions had created. Consequently, she lived in an atmosphere of emotional pain, depression, and hopelessness. The unfaithful, sinful actions of her husband had devastated her and her children. Sin always brings death and destruction. However, the Good News is, *Christ has overcome and defeated the power of sin* and offers us a future and a hope.

Neither the sinful behavior of others, nor our own past mistakes or failures have to control our future or the realms and atmospheres in which we live. We have a choice to make – we can either accept Christ's power to create heaven on earth, peacefully abide in Him, and allow His creative life to flow into us, or we can separate ourselves from His presence, wisdom, and encouragement by unbelief in His power or goodness.

Taming Daniel's Lions

Take Daniel, for example. He lived in the midst of an extremely oppressive environment. God's people had disobeyed and rebelled against Him for many years. In spite of many warnings and clear prophetic calls to righteousness, they had continued their evil ways. As a result, God placed them under the control of Babylon, the most brutal heathen nation of that day. By their choices and actions, they had actually sold themselves into bondage.

They lived in a horrible atmosphere of severe oppression, poverty, and hopelessness because they had departed from the Lord. Daniel was a young man who had not made the sinful choices that caused their judgment and yet he, too, was taken to Babylon. Although the consequences of their sin were all around him, they did not affect him. Daniel lived in a different realm and atmosphere; rather than defeat, he lived in the glory of God's goodness. Daniel created realms and atmospheres that were full of opportunities and testimonies.

While others of his nation were toiling under terrible oppression, Daniel was living in an environment of God's righteousness. He was a godly influence on the key leaders of his day, wrote glorious testimonies, had encounters with God, and created prophetic journals that eventually became part of the Bible. Even when unjustly put into a den with the lions, Daniel created

We have a choice to make – we can either accept Christ's power to create heaven on earth ... or we can separate ourselves from His presence, wisdom, and encouragement.

an atmosphere of peace through his trust in God, and the lions had to yield to Daniel's angel-enforced atmosphere. Wise choices and actions flowed from his love relationship with God to create realms and atmospheres of victory, purpose, and promise despite the difficult times and repressive environment in which he lived.

Like Daniel, you also can create environments of victory, purpose, promise, and testimony in the midst of your own lions of despair, darkness, and defeat.

Creating Portals of Blessing

Over the years, I have contended through faith for breakthrough in the various regions in which we have lived and ministered, and I have witnessed the glory of God settle there as a result.

We moved to Maricopa, Arizona, in 2005. The recession that began in 2007 hit our city hard. Reports say that our small community is one of those areas with a record number of houses in foreclosure. As a ministry, we knew we had to rise up in Kingdom authority to proclaim blessing over our city.

In Christ, believers have authority over the city in which they live. (Where you live is not an accident; God positioned you there to bring heaven to your corner of the earth.) The Lord moved in glorious ways for us during this time of recession and turned the devastated housing market into a blessing for many. Some people were able to purchase homes at low foreclosure prices; others got extremely reasonable rentals, and many church plants were established in the city.

Our prayer teams regularly go to the entrance points (the gates) of Maricopa and declare the protection, provision, and power of the Lord over our city. We have seen this type of authoritative prayer influence our region in amazing ways. One time, we caught wind of a strategy of the enemy regarding a violent bike gang that planned to move into our city to establish a base and clubhouse.

We heard through a reliable source that they would use it as a drug distribution center, and some of the club leaders would relocate here. When we became aware of this, we took a stand against it and declared in prayer, "NOT ON OUR WATCH!" We stood our ground in faith and tenacious intercession. Within a month, the gang had changed its mind and decided that our community was not suitable for them after all. Ha! God has given us authority; however, we must exercise it to see change occur.

As we were looking over the city's needs during the time of recession, I realized that it needed more businesses – Christ-centered businesses that would influence the city with God's goodness. One day during prayer, I was stirred with a creative idea to establish a hair salon that could offer employment, be a light for Christ, and bring encouragement to the city. A friend and I prayed in agreement and began calling forth that business in prayer. We can "call those things that were not as though they were" because like our God, we also have the right and ability to create with our words.

Soon, La Vida Hair Boutique was birthed. This sweet, humble outreach in the community touches many lives; it is a portal of blessing. We have so much fun watching as many receive refreshment and pleasure in the Lord through the hair salon, while God gives us continuous opportunities to touch hearts with His goodness and love.

We also saw the potential to use our salon as a portal of blessing to developing nations. Consequently, we have created an opportunity for our salon to make an impact in Cambodia by establishing a beauty school and salon to train girls rescued from the sex trade. In addition, we are giving funds from the Maricopa salon to minister to at-risk children in Cambodia. When we use our ability to create, we make "our world" a better place not only for ourselves but also for others.

This project might seem small and insignificant to some, but God celebrates small beginnings! We have always started with the *micro* and God has been faithful to breathe on it, creating waves of influence far beyond what we imagined – God turns the micro into macro.

A Media Portal

Years ago, I discovered that we could produce video media that could get the Good News out through the Internet. We produced a few short video clips and uploaded them – thousands watched those first videos.

Because of the success of our first efforts, we continued to build the video library and eventually created an entire network called XPmedia.com that hosts hundreds of ministry channels and reaches the world 24/7. Now millions of pages are viewed monthly and, wherever I go around the world, people tell me, "I watch you every day on the Internet." An apostolic leader who lives and ministers in a Muslim nation shared, "Your online media feeds my entire apostolic network of leaders. We do not know where we would be without it." That really blessed me. We began small but it grew and had a ripple effect in the nations. God gave us the inspiration, and we created it with Him and for Him. Now God has a channel of influence in the world through this network. I love creating with God … and you will, too!

Power to Create

You have been set apart as a *pure* vessel to release the Kingdom of God in the earth. You do not need to sit around and just hope for something good to happen; you can actually create that good. You do not need to wait for things to come into "divine order" before you act on your God-given authority to create. You can create order in the midst of chaos right *now*!

In Deuteronomy 8, the Lord was preparing His people to possess and occupy their "Promised Land." Verse 18 teaches that they had the "power to make" (create, obtain) wealth, "But you shall remember the Lord your God, for it is He who is **giving you power to make wealth**, that He may confirm His covenant …" (emphasis added).

The word "power" in Deuteronomy 8:18 refers to *man's* strength and ability when empowered by God. The word "make" refers to the action taken to implement, create, or obtain. God has given you the power to create wealth. However, when you use this power to create, you must never take the credit and forget it was He who empowered you.

Even though this Scripture refers specifically to the creation of wealth, you also have the power to create the manifestation of other promises of God in your life. You can create things like *favor* instead of rejection and *blessing* instead of curse. You can create *heaven on earth* in your marriage and *health* and *strength* in your body.

Although God has given you this ability, you must always acknowledge Him as its source. You can create His glory in the earth, but only by His enabling grace. He gave this sober warning in Deuteronomy 8:19, "If you ever forget the Lord your God and go after other gods and serve them and worship them, I testify against you today that you will surely perish."

*You are on the very threshold of creating
outrageous realms of goodness.*

God has given you the power and the ability to do so. He is with you to lead, guide, teach, and inspire – "Arise, shine; for your light has come, And the glory of the Lord has risen upon you" (Isaiah 60:1).

*Follow Him into the best years of your life …
this is your hour … this is your world!*

2

DEFINING REALMS AND ATMOSPHERES

2

DEFINING REALMS AND ATMOSPHERES

YOUR REALMS OF INFLUENCE DEFINE YOUR WORLD, and everyone has these realms. Your world includes everything in your life.

A Realm Is Defined as:

•   A *territory* (visible or invisible) over which rule or control is exercised, for example:

   An operations manager in a company can administer his or her realm of responsibility with a spirit of excellence.

   The worship of a congregation can activate angels in the unseen realm and cause many to experience supernatural encounters.

•   Something *dominant,* for example:

   A realm of success dominated the life of Mr. Jones.

   The realm of God's tangible glory prevailed in the meeting.

•   A *field of knowledge, activity, expertise,* for example:

   The neurologist was an expert in the realm of brain surgery.

   Mike Leonard was an icon in the realm of college football.

- A *sphere of interest or concern,* for example:

  In the realm of history, you see a consistent pattern of pride bringing ruin.

  The Parent Teacher Association raised concerns regarding realms of misbehavior in the school.

- An *atmosphere,* for example:

  There was a realm of peace in the room that brought a calming influence.

  The arguments in the meeting created a realm of turmoil.

Your realms are everything you influence, rule over, and give form or shape to in your life. For example, the house you live in is a part of your realm of influence. You have stewardship over it because it is part of your domain. Other common realms of influence are your workplace, church, relationships, family, and finances. Your realms also include your spiritual gifts and talents, hobbies, health, and academic interests. You have God-given authority *to rule* over and steward each of your realms, as well as the God-given ability *to create* within your realms.

Your Realms of Influence Are "Your World."

Living in Two Realms

Jesus lived in two realms (dimensions or spheres) at the same time. In John chapter three, Jesus explained the realities of the Kingdom to Nicodemus. I am sure Nicky's religious foundations were shaken to the core when Jesus said, "No one has ascended into heaven, but He who came down from heaven (that is), the Son of Man who is in heaven" (John 3:13 NKJV).

Through this statement, Jesus explained that He lived in two realms or dimensions at the same time. Even though He was physically on earth talking to Nicodemus in the natural, earthly realm, He made this mysterious and perplexing statement, "The Son of Man *who IS in heaven*." He was in heaven and on earth at the same time. Jesus existed in both the realm of time and the realm of eternity. He interacted with the earthly realm and the heavenly realm simultaneously.

When Jesus healed the sick, He actually released health from the heavenly realm into the corrupted earthly realm. He created life-giving health in the midst of sickness and disease. All the miracles He performed were because He released the heavenly realm into the earthly.

Realms of Time and Eternity

Time is a created entity. God established time in Genesis chapter one when He created day and night. Time is a realm that lies within eternity. "Eternity" is hard to envision; I like to think of it as a massive expanse with no ceiling, floor, or walls; a realm that goes on forever, that always has been and always will be. I sometimes imagine "time" as a small capsule floating within "eternity."

Both eternity and time are separate realms. The eternal realm hosts God's holy heaven and Kingdom, and the realm of time hosts the earthly, natural dimension.

The Son of God, who is eternal, entered the realm of "time" through the incarnation. When you were born again, you received *eternal* life within your spirit, yet your physical body remained within the *natural realm* of "time." That means you are an eternal being with complete access to the eternal realm while living within the realm of time. You are both natural and spiritual. Paul described these two realms in 2 Corinthians 4:18:

> While we look not at the things which are seen, but the things which are not seen; for the things which are seen are temporal, but the things which are not seen are eternal.

The word *temporal* means "subject to time." It refers to the natural or earthly realm in which we live. *Eternal* refers to "the unseen, spiritual realm," the realm where God's heaven is located.

Like Jesus, you can also access both realms. Like Jesus, you can create eternal substance and qualities in the earthly realm in which you live. Jesus taught that He only did the things He saw His Father do (John 5:19) and taught us to pray, "Our Father who is [lives] *in heaven*" (Matthew 6:9, emphasis added). Jesus said He only did those things He saw His Father do. Since His Father lived in heaven, then Jesus had to access the heavenly realm while functioning and living on earth.

Many believers think of the heavenly realm as if it was "a galaxy far, far away" but actually it is quite close. It is only on the other side of the veil between the natural and invisible realms. You cannot measure the closeness of the unseen realm by using the concepts of time and distance because those measures are "natural." The spiritual realm is only a thought away.

You have access to the heavenly realm through the blood of Christ:

> Therefore, brethren, since we have confidence to enter the holy place by the blood of Jesus ... (Hebrews 10:19).

> He raised Him from the dead and seated Him at His right hand in the heavenly places ... and raised us up with Him, and seated us with Him in the heavenly places in Christ Jesus (Ephesians 1:20; 2:6).

Paul further confirms your access to the heavenly, eternal dimension in Ephesians 1 and 2. You are currently seated in heavenly places "in Christ," at the right hand of the Father with full access to that realm – even though your body is in the earthly realm. Because you are "in Christ," you can live and operate in both realms.

Jesus said we who believe in Him would do the same works He did, and He stated that as the Father sent Him into the world, He has also sent us (John 14:12; 20:21). Jesus only did things He saw His Father in heaven do, and you can function in the same way. Like Jesus, you have full access to your Father in the heavenly realm with the ability and assignment to implement His will in the earth. As a citizen of heaven, according to Ephesians 2:19, you, like Jesus, are a heavenly being who lives on the earth.

You can cause the glory of heaven to invade your realms of influence in the earth. In Christ, you can literally "create heaven on earth!"

Atmospheres

Following are definitions[1] of *atmosphere*:

1. A general pervasive feeling or mood: an *atmosphere* of elation

2. A special mood or character associated with a place

Atmospheres include the actual tone of your life or a situation. You can feel atmospheres. For example, you might walk into a church meeting and feel an atmosphere of faith or the atmosphere of the presence of the Lord. You can possibly sense the atmosphere of anticipation. The same is true of the opposite. I have walked into meetings where there was a clear atmosphere of skepticism and

---

[1]Dictionary.com

unbelief. You could feel it in the air. The doubts and fears of those in attendance created this atmosphere.

In one meeting, I discerned the atmosphere of unbelief and knew I had to create faith in the room for God's purposes to be fulfilled that evening. The Holy Spirit inspired me to prophesy and bring words of knowledge over some of the individuals in the meeting. As I did, anticipation grew and the atmosphere in the room changed from unbelief to faith. Once faith was present, I could fulfill the assignment the Lord had given me. An atmospheric shift took place as I followed the Lord's leading to create faith in a meeting where unbelief, doubt, and skepticism had prevailed.

We can actually transform the entire world when we engage in our God-appointed call to create realms and atmospheres of His Kingdom in our areas of influence. You need not wait!

I once visited a home so filled with strife and contention that I could feel it as I walked through the door. No one had said a word, but the atmosphere was charged with unrest. The thoughts, words, and actions of those in the home created that atmosphere. Atmospheres do not manifest on their own volition – they are created.

The power of God will always displace a negative atmosphere. There is no need to live in a home with a prevailing atmosphere of strife and contention. In Christ, you have the power to create an atmosphere of love, honor, respect, and humility. You can create atmospheric shifts.

I once ministered to a couple in a dilemma. The husband wanted to quit his job due to the unrighteous atmosphere that prevailed in his workplace. When he described the situation, I could empathize with him. The men he worked with constantly used foul language, shared perverted humor, mocked him continuously, and displayed porno on the walls where he worked. The hellish atmosphere vexed him every day. I challenged him to use his God-given power to create a righteous environment and to begin with his own workstation. He had power to create a righteous portal over his assigned place. After receiving some encouragement and "spiritual tools," he proceeded to activate his privilege to create with God. Within a short time, he noticed a difference. Initially, he was creating an atmosphere of purity and peace for himself, but before long, it began affecting and influencing others in the workplace. It was awesome! In Christ, you have the ability to create heavenly atmospheres in *your* world!

What an opportunity we have: we can actually transform the entire world when we engage in our God-appointed call to create realms and atmospheres of His Kingdom in our areas of influence. You need not wait!

You can begin right now to *create your world.*

In the coming chapters you will discover twelve practical keys for creating realms and atmospheres that will make your world wonderful and further the Kingdom of heaven on earth.

3

KEY #1—THE POWER OF KNOWING WHO YOU ARE!

3

KEY #1—THE POWER OF KNOWING WHO YOU ARE!

MANY CHRISTIANS LIVE IN REALMS OF DEFEAT and unfruitfulness simply because they do not understand who God created them to be. They never step into creating a beautiful world around them simply because they do not know they can. It is vital that you understand who you are *in Christ*, so let's explore the Scriptures together, embrace important truths, and find out who you really are!

Beginning at "the Beginning"

In Genesis 1:1-3, the Scriptures declare that in the beginning when the world was without form and void (actually meaning "in a state of formlessness, confusion, and chaos")[2] God spoke into the darkness and said, "Let there be light"… and there was light.

Every time you see the word **God** in the account of creation in Genesis 1 and 2, it is the Hebrew word *Elohiym* meaning "Ruler or Divine One," referring to God, our Creator. The word *created* in Genesis 1:1 means "to form, shape, and create."

---

[2]From Strong's Lexicon of Hebrew Words (1) formlessness, confusion, unreality, emptiness, formlessness (of primeval earth), wilderness, chaos.

God is indeed the divine Ruler and Creator of all things. The essence of His being fills all eternity, and no being in the universe can ever come near to matching His divine majesty, authority, power, and creativity. He alone is altogether perfect, flawless in nature, and eternal. The attributes of ruling and creating are part of His very nature. Through His creative power, He spoke order into chaos. He created something where there was nothing, light where there was darkness, and form in the midst of disorder.

Reading further in Genesis, we discover that God (Elohiym) created mankind in His image and likeness and blessed them to rule and reign in the earth:

God [Elohiym – Ruler and Creator] created man in His own image, in the image of God [Elohiym – Ruler and Creator] He created him; male and female He created them. God [Elohiym – Ruler and Creator] blessed them; and God [Elohiym – Ruler and Creator] said to them, "Be fruitful and multiply, and fill the earth, and subdue it; and rule over the fish of the sea and over the birds of the sky and over every living thing that moves on the earth" (Genesis 1:27-28).

This is a powerful statement and a very important revelation that defines who *you* are. You were made in the very image and likeness of the divine Ruler and Creator – God (Elohiym). This means that God gave you the ability to rule over, and create within, your God-given realm of influence. You could say that you are His little "elohiym." God's original intention, before the fall of man, was for you to be His "ruler" and "creator" in the earth realm.

Psalm 82:6 says, "You are gods, and all of you are sons of the Most High." The word used for "gods" in this verse is "elohiym." Remember, however, that no human is comparable to our God (Elohiym), and no being will ever be able to usurp Him – never! He is fully sovereign, omnipotent, omniscient, and omnipresent, BUT He created you with His "DNA." You were made in His image and likeness, therefore, His abilities abide in you through the Spirit of Christ. Perfection, power, and love are within your new nature, and eternal life is your gift from Him. You cannot earn it and you cannot produce it with human effort.

Who Owns and Who Manages the Garden?

Psalm 24:1 explains, "The earth is the Lord's, and all it contains, the world, and those who dwell in it." However, Psalm 115:16 clarifies that God gave man dominion over the earth, "The heavens are the heavens of the Lord, but the earth He has given to the sons of men."

This means that we, mankind, were given "stewardship" of the earth. We walk with God to manage, oversee, and protect the world in which we live. Man makes choices in the earth that determine either its well-being or destruction.

The fall of mankind is recorded in Genesis soon after the account of creation. Through Adam's disobedience to God, mankind became subject to the enemy. Even the birthright of rule and authority God had given man became subject to Satan. Paul explains in Romans 6:16 that we become slaves to the one we submit ourselves to:

> Do you not know that when you present yourselves to someone as slaves for obedience, you are slaves of the one whom you obey, either of sin resulting in death, or of obedience resulting in righteousness.

When Adam and Eve chose to sin, they accepted the enemy's lie over God's truth and became slaves to the liar, Satan. A slave has no authority over his environment; consequently, man surrendered his God-given authority over the earth to the enemy of God and man.

This does not mean that mankind was completely unable to rule or create. After the Fall, both men and women were creating, pro-creating, and leading realms of influence. However, they had lost their God-given appointment and the full extent of their power to exercise God's righteous authority in the earth, because they now lived under the authority of sin. Mankind had no choice but to remain under bondage to Satan, the "god of this world," until Christ completed His work on the Cross.

God, in His goodness, had a plan to return us to His original intent. What a glorious gift and relief! Jesus Christ, who is fully God and fully Man, made possible our restoration to our original status of sons and daughters of God authorized to rule in the earth. By His death on the Cross for the sins of all mankind and His victory over Satan, hell, and death, we can now reclaim our former authority. To gain access to all that Jesus accomplished, however, we must be "in Christ." This means we must ask for forgiveness of sin and make Him Lord of our lives.

The Great Commission – It's More Than You Think

God knew that we could not keep His ways (successfully live by the Law) so He decided to fulfill both sides of His eternal covenant with man. He carried out not only all of His terms of the covenant but also all of man's terms through Christ. When Jesus came to earth, He did not come as God, even though He was God. He came as a man – a Perfect Man like Adam at his creation. The Bible calls Him the "last Adam" in 1 Corinthians 15:45.

On our behalf, He won back our authority and was able to say to His disciples and to all believers:

All authority has been given to Me in heaven and on earth. Go therefore and **make disciples of all the nations**, baptizing them in the name of the Father and the Son and the Holy Spirit, **teaching them to observe all that I commanded you**; and lo, I am with you always, even to the end of the age (Matthew 28:18-20, emphasis added).

I will give you the keys of the kingdom of heaven; and **whatever you bind on earth shall have been bound in heaven, and whatever you loose on earth shall have been loosed in heaven** (Matthew 16:19, emphasis added).

Behold, **I have given you authority** to tread on serpents and scorpions, and **over all the power of the enemy**, and nothing will injure you (Luke 10:19, emphasis added).

I have put in bold the parts of the foregoing verses that emphasize that Jesus received all power and authority and then gave it to His people to bring the Kingdom of heaven to the nations. We are to fill the earth with His truth, making disciples of all the nations.

In Christ, you possess and must use the "Keys of the Kingdom" to create God's purposes and desires in the earth. You hold the keys of His authority and have the power *in Christ* to "bind"[3] in the earth with heaven's backing. You can also "loose"[4] in the earth and heaven will confirm it. Everything that Jesus settled through the finished work of the Cross is now established and celebrated in heaven. He completely defeated the enemy for you. Therefore, you can bind any demonic interference in your life and loose the righteous will of God into your midst, because on the Cross, Jesus overcame all sin and works of the devil. You can also take dominion over your

---

[3] To *bind* means to tie up, to fasten, to keep from straying, to keep inoperative (Strong's Concordance, Webster's Dictionary, Oxford Dictionary)

[4] To *loose* means to release and to undo; to untie (Strong's Concordance, Webster's Dictionary, Oxford Dictionary)

internal enemy, the flesh, win on the battlefield of the mind, and loose the nature of God into your life ... the Lord will back you up!

The blessing God proclaimed over mankind in Genesis 1:27-28 now refers to Christ and those "in Him!" If Jesus is your Savior, you are in Christ, and these Scriptures refer to you! You are recreated in Christ to rule and create in your world just like your Father, Elohiym. Under His commanded blessing, you *will* be fruitful and multiply! Heaven is waiting for us to take back dominion in the earth. God is waiting for His children to understand their legacy, take their place, exercise their rule, and reign with Him on the earth.

We have full access to the heavenly dimensions, and God has granted us "everything that pertains to life and to godliness."[5] Through these gifts, we can co-labor and rule with Him in the earth. We have all we need to live in the image and likeness of Elohiym, our God. With these gifts, we can take possession of our individual and corporate destinies.

> Oftentimes, we have waited for God to bring order into our chaos or light to our darkest hour when *He is waiting* for us to take control of the situation.

This is extremely important for believers to understand: Oftentimes, we have waited for God to bring order into our chaos or light to our darkest hour when *He is waiting* for us to take control of the situation. The enemy no longer has the "right" by way of authority to be in charge of the world. However, he will not leave of his own volition. We are to unseat him by removing him from his places of authority in our lives, our culture, and the world.

---

[5]Hebrews 9:24; 10:19-22; 12:18-24; 2 Peter 1:2-4; Ephesians 1:3

We can no longer sit back just hopin' and prayin' that God will show up and change our world. He "showed up" two thousand years ago and now waits for us to activate our God-given authority and ability to create with Him the Kingdom of God on the earth. Creation is even waiting for us to take our place.[6]

Help! Help! Help!

Jesus is no longer on the earth; He is seated at the right hand of the Father, waiting for us to execute His purposes on the earth. However, He did not leave us all alone to accomplish our mission. God sent the Holy Spirit, the very Spirit of Christ, to lead and guide us into all truth and to strengthen and support us. In this way, we are *in Christ*, seated with Him at the right hand of the Father. And He is in us through His Spirit in the earth, entwined with Him in both realms:

> But I tell you the truth, it is to your advantage that I go away; for if I do not go away, the Helper will not come to you; but if I go, I will send Him to you ... I have many more things to say but you cannot bear them now. But when He, the Spirit of truth comes, He will guide you into all truth; for He will not speak on His own initiative, but whatever He hears, He will speak; and He will disclose to you what is to come (John 16:7,12-13).

YOU ARE NEVER ALONE! (Read those four words again and again until they become your personal proverb.) The Spirit of Jesus is with you to lead and empower you to create realms and atmospheres that are blessed with the glory of God. The Holy Spirit loves walking with you and invites you to walk with Him! This invitation is irresistible – oh, how marvelous!

---

[6]Romans 8:19-21

In Christ, YOU are the Gate!

Genesis 28:10-17 tells about Jacob's dream of a ladder. In that dream, he saw a ladder set on the earth with a top that reached to heaven. Angels were ascending and descending, and the Lord was standing above it. When Jacob woke up from the dream, he said:

Surely **the Lord is in this place**, and I did not know it … How awesome is this place. This is none other than the **house of God** and this is the **gate of heaven** (Genesis 28:16-17, emphasis added).

This dream is a prophetic picture of the body of Christ. We are the "house of God" and, according to 1 Corinthians 6:19, the "temple of the Holy Spirit." The Lord is in "this place," this "house" – *us*! Have you ever thought of yourself as a "house" or "gate"? Consider this: you house the very presence of God in the earth because His Spirit dwells within you. Jesus taught that He was the entrance to the Kingdom, and Scripture refers to Him as the gate or door to eternal life, and now He lives in you! When you truly believe this, you will begin to live life differently and discover what Jesus meant when He promised believers the abundant life in John 10:10.

You are a powerhouse because you house the God of power!

Because of your heavenly access, you can literally bring the blessings of heaven to earth, just as Jesus did during His ministry on earth. (We study this subject in greater detail in our Glory School – see featured items in back of this book).

You Are a King and a Priest

Revelation 1:6 describes your appointment as "kings and priests" unto God: "[He] has made us kings and priests to His God and Father, to Him *be* glory and dominion forever and ever" (NKJV).

A king is one who rules, and a priest is one who stands in the gap between heaven and earth. You are the king of your domain. You are the ruler (under Christ's authority) over your life and the affairs of your life. You also represent Christ's kingly authority wherever He leads you to execute it in the nations.

The word "priest" in this passage does not refer to a clergyperson in a religious order, but rather the job of believers in Christ to minister to God in worship and intercession. A born-again priest calls forth God's purposes into the earth and gives Him honor from the earth (1 Peter 2:9). As a royal Kingdom priest, you:

1. Worship God (John 4:23-24).

2. Offer gifts to Him (Hebrews 5:1).

3. Stand before Him in intercession on behalf of man (Hebrews 7:25).

4. Exercise your power in Christ to remit sins (John 20:23).

5. Invite God's intervention into situations that need to be touched by His Kingdom (Matthew 6:10).

6. Co-labor with God to pray for His will to manifest in the earth (Matthew 6:10).

7. Stand against Satan and his works on behalf of others and war for their freedom (Luke 10:19).

Christ is the eternal High Priest, the Priest of all priests and King of all kings. Your presence on earth as king and priest is vitally important. As both king and priest, you will advance the Kingdom of God in the earth by stewarding your realms. God created you for this purpose.

A Review

To be prepared for the next chapters, it is important to become established in the fundamental principles of this chapter and the preceding ones. You must know with certainty that you have the ability to influence your spheres of authority in the earth because of who you are "in Christ." Study carefully the following review:

1. You were made in the image of God (Elohiym – Ruler, Creator) – Genesis 1:27.

2. In Christ, you have access into the heavenly realms and can bring the will and atmosphere of heaven to earth – Hebrews 10:19, Matthew 6:10.

3. You can bind and loose in the earth because you possess the Keys of the Kingdom – Matthew 16:19.

4. God has given you stewardship of the earth in Christ – Psalm 115:16.

5. You are a king and a priest unto God and therefore can rule over your domain and stand in the gap for the purposes of God to enter the earth – Revelation 1:6.

Ready for more? Let's discover Key #2.

4

KEY #2—THE POWER OF ABIDING IN CHRIST

4

Key #2—The Power of Abiding in Christ

I AM THE TRUE VINE, and My Father is the vinedresser. Every branch in Me that does not bear fruit, He takes away; and every *branch* that bears fruit, He prunes it so that it may bear more fruit. You are already clean because of the word which I have spoken to you. Abide in Me, and I in you. As the branch cannot bear fruit of itself unless it abides in the vine, so neither *can* you unless you abide in Me. I am the vine, you are the branches; he who abides in Me and I in him, he bears much fruit, for apart from Me you can do nothing. If anyone does not abide in Me, he is thrown away as a branch and dries up; and they gather them, and cast them into the fire and they are burned. If you abide in Me, and My words abide in you, ask whatever you wish, and it will be done for you (John 15:1-7).

Jesus said *if we abide in Him we would bear much fruit*. However, *without Him we can do nothing*. We have an orange tree in our back-yard that yields enormous amounts of fruit. The branches host the fruit but do not strive to bring it forth; they simply abide in the tree. That's right! All they do is enjoy the sun, the refreshing rain, and allow the sap from the tree to flow through them. When it is time to bear fruit, they do! Merely by being branches, they become loaded with fruit, because orange trees produce oranges.

No matter how hard an orange tree branch might try, it can never create even one orange on its own. In addition, if it becomes separated from the tree, it will wither and die. When unconnected to its source, death is the outcome, because a branch by itself has no power to create life. It will, however, produce death when it fails to abide in the tree.

With this in mind, you can see how the life you currently live is the result of the source to which you connect yourself. When you abide in Christ, you have creative power flowing through you, like sap flowing through a tree to its branches. As you "hang with Jesus" and allow His Spirit and Word to direct, you will see godly, eternal fruit created in every aspect of life that pertains to you.

Striving? or Abiding?

When I was first born again, I was completely captured by God's love. I literally felt the power of the Lord's love remove my sin, guilt, and shame on the night I gave my life to Jesus. Oh, it was so glorious! I did nothing to deserve it. I can't even claim to have found Him, He apprehended me.

The first few years of my walk with Him, I enjoyed complete joy and rest in Him as He graciously led me into paths of mercy and righteousness. I did not have a desire to sin and I was not sin-conscious. I only wanted to be with Him. I arose early in the morning hours, before the rest of the household, just to seek Him. I stayed up late at night soaking in His presence and studying His Word. This was not because I felt a pressure to seek Him, but because my heart longed for more of Him. His love and presence was so irresistible; He was my desire. My thoughts were on Him constantly and, as a result, my life bore fruit – with ease. The blessing of the Lord abounded, and He blessed me with the privilege of leading many souls to Christ, ministering healing and deliverance to the afflicted. I was blessed everywhere I turned. It was easy. I did not strive or struggle. When I read insights and instruction from the Word, I activated them – not because I felt a pressure to obey the Word, but because I wanted to.

Oh, I had been highjacked by Love Himself, and the more I hung out in His love presence the more I became like Him, bearing fruit on every branch of life.

After a few years of growing in the Lord, my husband and I were blessed with an opportunity to go to the mission field. As new babes in Christ, we had been mentored in a glorious environment of the grace of God and knew nothing about legalism. After a short time on the field working under leaders who emphasized works and striving rather than restful abiding, we were a mess. I was even questioning my salvation and wondered if God loved me. I thought that maybe He was angry with me.

This is what sin-conscious legalism will do to you. These leaders passionately loved the Lord and had laid down everything to serve Him. I love and honor them, as they are amazing individuals. But they did not understand the blessing of *restful abiding* versus the pressure of human striving. My husband and I did not know how to rightly divide the advice and teaching they were giving us, so we jumped into a net of deception that I never want to step into again – and I won't!

The Fruit of Legalism

The principles of the Word work because His law is perfect and awesome. On the other hand, the Bible says, "The letter kills, but the Spirit gives life" (2 Corinthians 3:6 NKJV). If we labor and strive to obey God's ways, then we have stepped into a legalistic mindset full of self-effort, and that is not part of our redemptive package. As we rest in Christ, we naturally live out what has already been accomplished through His finished work on the Cross, all without striving to accomplish it. I now walk in obedience to the Word, not because I *must,* but because I love the Word and with joy I *get to* discover its glorious benefits and fruit.

We were rescued from the deception, and our experience with legalism was short lived (Praise the Lord!). As we see in Genesis 3 when Adam and Eve fell from grace, we cannot eat the fruit of legalism or we shall surely die! We simply need to abide in Christ.

Some of the manifestations of abiding in the law rather than in Christ are:

1. Loss of joy
2. Loss of childlike faith and trust in God
3. Inability to accept failure in others
4. Bitterness, offense, and unforgiveness
5. Striving
6. Feeling distanced and separated from God
7. Lack of peace
8. Anxiety

If you find yourself experiencing any of these manifestations, take time to find your rest in Christ. As you soak in His love, He will teach and inspire you. As you follow His leading in "rest," you will be amazed at how much fruit you bear!

What's Your Posture?

You can find a great example of *abiding* in the New Testament account of Martha and Mary:

Now as they were traveling along, He entered a village; and a woman named Martha welcomed Him into her home. She had a sister called Mary, who was seated at the Lord's feet, listening to His word. But Martha was distracted with all her preparations; and she came up *to Him* and said, "Lord, do You not care that my sister has left me to do all the serving alone? Then tell her to help me." But the Lord answered and said to her, "Martha, Martha, you are worried and bothered about so many things; but *only* one thing is necessary, for Mary has chosen the good part, which shall not be taken away from her" (Luke 10:38-42).

Mary was sitting at His feet – restfully abiding, listening to His words, and absorbing them. Martha, however, was striving to please Him and became oh so frustrated. However, Jesus celebrated Mary's posture because it would bring forth fruit.

I have discovered that amazing grace always flows from the posture of restful abiding in Him. That is the source for joy and enormous measures of fruit. Like Mary, drink in His goodness and enjoy His unconditional love for you. Soak in His kindness, and as He reveals things to act upon, do them with joy and the fruit will appear. It's that easy.

Your ability to create comes from abiding in Christ

If you do not understand abiding and living in the revelation of the gospel of His love, then read my book, *God Loves You with an Everlasting Love* until the revelation hits you. (I have included this short book at the end of this book.) You will discover that it is easy to abide in Him when you know His unconditional love and favor for you. The gospel of His love is so glorious it will transform you!

5

KEY #3—THE POWER OF WORSHIP AND DEVOTION

5

Key #3—The Power of Worship and Devotion

*Whoever or whatever you worship
defines your realms and atmospheres.*

DEVOTION is defined as "profound dedication or consecration."

WORSHIP means "the acknowledgement given by a servant to his lord." Worship involves extravagant adoration.

Most who read this book will think that devotion to God and worship of Him is a settled issue in their hearts. Jesus is their Lord and Savior, the One they worship. However, even born-again believers have other things that pull on their hearts, things that demand their devotion and worship. Let me explain.

Bling in Tinsel Town

It has been my privilege to know many wonderful, humble, and committed Christian people in the entertainment industry. They are truly amazing and their character is outstanding. However, one day during some business meetings in Hollywood, I sensed an unpleasant *atmosphere* that disturbed me. There seemed to be an air of one-upmanship that included things like name-dropping, boasting, flaunting of pricey handbags, and subtle innuendos that revealed motivations of pride and selfish ambition. They made me feel uncomfortable.

Later that evening, I mentioned that I was wrestling with these prideful *atmospheres* to Shirley Ross, my television producer and close friend who had accompanied me. I asked her to help me unpack my feelings. She had lived in the Hollywood area and worked in the film industry for more than twenty-two years before laying it all down to serve the Lord with me in Christian media.

With great transparency, Shirley revealed that she had also "put on airs" during her time of working in the industry. She explained that it was never really her focus to have lots of money, fame, or recognition merely for the sake of those things. Instead, her pretentious behavior resulted from a longing to be valued and affirmed. Those in her social circle believed that driving an expensive car, living in a prestigious neighborhood, wearing designer fashions, carrying expensive handbags, taking exotic vacations, making excessive incomes on contracts, and personally knowing "who's who in the Hollywood zoo" made you a person of value and worth.

She shared that the desire for all those "things" is actually a quest for value and worth for most individuals. She further explained that many in her industry struggle with the "fear of disqualification" and that she personally knew of some who had literally sold their souls to the devil to ensure their upward climb on the ladder of success. However, when they finally "arrived," they were disillusioned and empty. They found that the very thing they believed would finally establish their worth and value actually left them confused, numb, alienated from others, and sometimes completely devastated.

> *Whatever you depend upon to provide self-worth*
> *becomes your idol.*

That was eye opening for me. I clearly understood the danger of looking for self-esteem, affirmation, value, protection, and assurance in things that ultimately can never deliver them. Whatever you depend on to establish your worth becomes your god or idol and even becomes your object of worship.

Could Gold Be Your God?

If you believe that money gives you worth, then the "love of money" will be your idol and the object of your "worship." Obtaining more and more money will consume your thinking, and this longing will be the focus of your affections. Your life or "world" will be entirely about making money and the "things" it can buy. Money, in that case, has become your god because you look to it to give you value and to fulfill your desires and needs.

Those who serve the "love of money" are never satisfied because they are empty even when they have abundance.

During the Great Depression and other times of economic crisis, men and women actually committed suicide when they lost all their assets. Because their "world" was all about their money, when it was gone their world ended.

In 2008, during the housing crisis, a woman approached me at a meeting asking for prayer. Her husband was worried about financial and real estate losses and, because of his fear, had gone into a deep depression. She said that the *atmosphere* of their home was so gloomy that she did not want to be there anymore. Her husband had idolized material possessions and derived his worth from them. He worshipped his assets and when his idol fell, so did his state of mind. The fall created a negative shift in the *atmosphere* of their home and family relationships. She was struggling in her marriage because of the gloomy spiritual *atmosphere* in their household.

Could Success Be Your Sweetheart?

Whoever or whatever has your heart's affection and adoration (worship) will create and determine your *realms*. For example, if you believe that success in a career is what will give you value and worth, then career focus will permeate every area of your life. The meditations of your mind will be about your career, and this focus will dominate most of your conversations. You will make decisions based on your drive for success, and those decisions will create *realms* and *atmospheres*.

I knew a man whose worth was so wrapped up in his career that it absorbed all his focus. Even though he had a wife and three children, he seldom spent time with them. Even during family dinners, his head would be in his computer, working on career-related projects, while his wife and children ate in complete silence. He would not allow conversation because it would disturb him from his work. After dinner, he made phone calls and prepared for his next day at work. His world was his work and he considered everything else extraneous.

> Those who serve the "love of money" are never satisfied because they are empty even when they have abundance.

It is not wrong to focus on success in your career, unless your quest for success determines your value and worth as a person. Then that focus has become an idol, and idols demand more and more of your attention and energy until they consume you and eventually destroy the truly important things in your life.

In this particular case, the worship of a career idol created a successful career but also produced an *atmosphere* of loneliness and disappointment at home. The children wanted and needed more of their father's attention, but it was not to be found. His wife longed for time with a caring husband, but his "idol" made that impossible. He was a great success at work but an abject failure at home.

Fruit of the Desire for Recognition

An individual's desire for prestige and recognition can become an idol. They believe that they will have worth and value if people of importance or influence affirm them. This type of focus can produce the fruit of self-centeredness, pride, and even cause the exploitation of others. Some might discern an *atmosphere* of arrogance around them. Ultimately, those who they trust in to give affirmation will fail them, because all idols eventually fall.

Adoration of Personal Appearance

Some worship their appearance. They believe that if they were just a little more beautiful or handsome then they would have more value. Many women idolize beauty and they are focused on their appearance. Some women are having plastic surgeries, implants, and other beauty enhancing procedures to feel esteemed as women. Appearance is also becoming the focus for some men who become obsessed with weight training and spending time at the gym. The focus on appearance permeates the *atmosphere* of their lives. None of these things is sinful or wrong in themselves, but if the treatments and activities are serving an idolatrous belief, then they will inevitably disappoint and fail over time.

According to Psalm 139, you were "fearfully and wonderfully made." You are beautiful to God just as you are. Your worth and value is found in God, your Creator. When you worship Him as the One who establishes your value in all things, His presence will fill the *realms* of your life. He is perfect in all His ways, all-wise, forever righteous, loving, kind, and full of beauty and glory. When you worship Him and make Him your *only* God, His beauty will prevail over aspects that you see as flaws, and His goodness will manifest in your physical appearance. Isaiah 60:2 says, "His glory will appear upon you."

Addictions Are Gods, Too

Over the years, I have ministered to many addicts. Regardless of the nature of the addiction, substance abuse, or obsessive behavior, it is an idol. Once addicted, you become capable of lying, deceiving, and possibly even stealing from those close to you. Addicts protect and defend their addictions. Although every form of addiction produces a different focus of worship (adoration), for the most part, addicts find their comfort, peace, joy, protection, and strength to face life or pain through their addiction. Their addiction becomes their life and identity.

Ultimately, the idols of addiction fail and destroy them. Most addicts eventually lose everything. I know countless numbers of addicts who have lost respect, finances, family relationships, marriages, friends, houses, jobs, personal peace, and health, yet they hold onto their addictions for dear life. They created *realms* of destruction, deception, and darkness in their lives by giving these substances their worship. The fruit of their addictions defines their lives. They worship the substance of their addiction.

"Yucky Spirits" That Make Your Head Swirl

A number of years ago, I was considering purchasing an investment home and a realtor took me to view some potential properties. When I walked into one of the homes, I was jolted in my spirit. My head began to swirl and I felt very strange all over. In the living room, I noticed statues of eastern gods and idols, along with an altar to them. Every room had similar elements indicating there was worship of these gods. It was evident that the owners of this home were devout worshippers of their idols. The influence of their gods created an oppressive *atmosphere*. (They must have been very dark spirits because their presence was disgusting.) Even though the homeowners were not present, the influence of the god they worshipped saturated the *atmosphere*.

God or the gods you worship create the atmosphere in YOUR home, too!

A Blast of Glory

I have a prayer room and study in my home where I sometimes lock myself for a few hours of worship and prayer. One day after an extended worship and prayer time, I left to get a cup of coffee from the kitchen. When I returned, the glory of the presence of the Lord in the room blasted me. I had been worshipping Jesus and His presence came and filled my room. I closed the door and returned to focusing on Him. Later, a friend knocked on the door to my study and I invited her in. When she walked into the room, she, too, was blasted by the glory of His presence. The *atmosphere* of heavenly peace, love, and glory fills our entire home because we worship the God of peace, love, and glory in that place. Some people have seen angels in our home, had God-encounters, gotten visions, and experienced dreams. Worship opened the heavenly *realms* in our dwelling and it will do the same in yours.

You always attract what or whomever you worship. If you worship Jesus and His Kingdom, that is who you will attract.

As an itinerant minister, I travel a lot and spend many weeks of the year in various hotel rooms around the world. I make it my practice upon entering a hotel room to invite the presence of the Lord to come and fill the room. His presence is full of light and love and, therefore, His light and love fills the *atmosphere* of the room – no matter where the room is or what has transpired there previously. The God I worship determines the *atmosphere* in which I live.

You always attract what or whomever you worship. If you worship Jesus and celebrate His Kingdom, that is what you will attract. Places of worship draw the very presence of Jesus and His angels.

Establishing Realms of His Presence

Our ministry once purchased a building that had previously been used as a house of worship for a cult, and later an atheist businessman had obtained the building. When the purchase closed, we immediately cleansed the land and the building from the defilement, through several means – with various prayers, deliverance ministry practices, and by worshipping there with our team. I put CD players in every room and continuously played worship songs that honored Jesus. We established a day of twenty-four hour worship and prayer in the building every month for a time, and we hosted worship and prayer proclamations outside the building.

At first, we did not notice a significant change in the spiritual *atmosphere*. It was still slightly oppressive and we knew that we had not yet established the tangible *realm* of glory. We continued to worship, soak, decree, and pray. Each time we worshipped we felt further breakthrough until the day finally came that a flood of God's glory entered the room. We had consecrated the building to Jesus and His holy purposes. Following that breakthrough, we had amazing encounters, miracles, signs, wonders, and even angelic visitations in that building. From that time on, there was always a lingering presence of the glory. At last, a *realm* of His presence was established.

Eventually, we built a TV studio in the sanctuary and the Word of the Lord went to the nations from that building. Jesus, who we worshipped, came and made that building a dwelling place for His presence through worship.

The *realm* that we created continued to expand and eventually influenced our city. The blessing of our ministry affected the leaders in the community as well as the general population. We proclaimed Jesus and worshipped Him as Lord, not only over our ministry but also over our city ... and God began to fill our city with His presence.

As we worshipped over strategic places of government, business, and education, we created *atmospheres* of heavenly authority.

> As we worshipped over strategic places of government, business, and education, we created *atmospheres* of heavenly authority.

Mixed Up in Mexico

During an outreach in Mexico many years ago, we became hopelessly lost on our way to a ministry assignment amongst the poor. The van was filled with ministry team members and it became very hot and uncomfortable. At every turn, we were more deeply trapped in a maze of unnamed streets. This was before cell phones and navigation systems. We were late for our ministry engagement and everyone was getting anxious and cranky. I finally said, "Let's stop the van and worship."

As we worshipped, the peace of God's presence came and the *atmosphere* in the van became one of glory rather than frustration.

Worship changed the *atmosphere*. Not long after we began worshipping, someone knocked on our window. It was one of the missionaries from the church. They had felt led of the Spirit to go out and look for us. They invited us to follow them to the venue. Our worship had created a *realm* for the Lord to fill. In His presence, there is fullness of joy.

In His presence, there is always clarity, direction,
wisdom, and guidance.

Brain Freeze

One day while working at my desk, I came to a point of discouragement due to a "brain freeze" or mental block. I needed answers and solutions to an administrative challenge but they continued to elude me. I could not seem to collect my thoughts and work through the issues I faced.

After numerous frustrating and failed attempts at drafting solutions for implementation, I decided to put my work down and worship. I sat back in my chair, turned my focus toward God, and worshipped Him as the all-wise God full of knowledge, counsel, understanding, and wisdom. I gave adoration for His brilliant mind that solves every problem. After a few moments of worship, I sensed His presence enter the room – a *realm* of His peace had opened. I continued to go deeper into worship and thanksgiving, declaring how wonderful He is! After enjoying this encounter for a while, I went back to work. Within moments, I had the download of wisdom I needed and the problems were completely solved.

I opened up a realm of wisdom through worship
and you can do the same.

Strategic Worship

Sometimes I "strategically worship" a particular attribute of God's nature. In your realms, you can create, enhance, or increase the specific aspect of God's nature and character that you worship. One day I was feeling very frustrated and anxious, my thoughts were negative and there was a swirl of tension around me. My unchecked anxiety had created a negative *atmosphere*. I thought about God's peace and remembered that He is never anxious about anything.

After deciding to quiet my mind, I sat in a chair in my living room and began to worship Him as the "God of Peace." My change of focus changed the *atmosphere*. As I adored Him for His great peace, He manifested His presence, and the essence of His peace flooded my mind, emotions, body, and the whole room. Suddenly, the thing that frustrated me became as nothing and God's presence prevailed. You can actually bring the atmosphere of heaven to earth!

A ministry friend of mine walks in a perpetual *realm* of peace. He constantly meditates on God's peace. Whenever he feels a lack of peace, he turns his focus back to God, and adores and worships the "God of all Peace." Before coming to Christ, he had a horrific upbringing with many painful challenges that were emotionally distressing and mentally disturbing. However, through worshipping and adoring the God of all Peace, he created a massive *realm* of peace surrounding his life. When he walks into a room, peace walks in with him.

You can change your atmosphere
by changing your focus.

Worship God as Provider, Create a Realm of Provision

Once when we were in the midst of a ministry building project, a massive unexpected expense hit us. Our budget was already tight and this surprise obligation really caught me off guard. Initially, I reacted with concern because I was uncertain how we could come up with the needed funds. I called our accountant and asked for bank balances and other information, but reviewing them only brought further apprehension. No matter how I tried to "crunch" the numbers, there was no way *in the natural* to meet this need. Oh, if only I had first worshipped my God of all Provision. He is so wonderful and glorious, and He deserves our *first* reaction. However, my response was to become anxious; yet God is gracious and merciful beyond measure.

When our team got together to pray about this need, I received a nudge from the Holy Spirit to simply worship God, since there was nothing we could do about the problem. I began to worship God's greatness as my Provider, a glorious Banker who meets all our needs. After only a few moments of worship, faith rose up in my heart and I began to call forth miracle provision from the north, south, east, and west. From that time on, I left things in God's hands. Whenever I felt tempted to be anxious, I worshipped Him for His greatness in the *realm* of provision. Within three weeks, He had met every need ... a realm of great provision had been created. We cannot even figure out how it happened, it just did!

Worship created a realm for miracle provision.

I find worshipping God irresistible because He is so amazing. We love Him because He first loved us. How can you not worship such a loving and kind God? He is all we need, He is more than enough. Oh, how lovely He is. Worship is a natural response when you live with a revelation of how glorious He is.

Some people exercise worship as a spiritual discipline, and I am not against that. At times, we need to enter into the sacrifice of praise and, like David, command our soul to bless the Lord in the midst of difficult circumstances. However, the very heart of our worship must flow from seeing Him as He is – the Lover of our soul.

Oh beloved reader, spend time in His presence gazing upon His unconditional love for you. When you drink of His love, worship is the natural response that flows freely from a grateful heart. That beautiful flow of worship creates heaven wherever you may be.

When you drink of His love, worship is the natural response that flows freely from a grateful heart.

Through heartfelt worship in response to God's love, I have experienced breakthroughs with health challenges, financial pressures, spiritual oppression, time delays on projects, and communication problems. Worship opens *realms* of healing, provision, love, wisdom, acceleration, and oh so much more.

To change any atmosphere, begin to worship God, because you create realms and atmospheres through your worship and adoration.

6

Key #4—The Power to Create Through Your Beliefs

6

Key #4—The Power to Create Through Your Beliefs

YOUR WORLD IS CREATED BY WHAT YOU BELIEVE – your perspective on life creates your realms. For example, those who believe they are failures actually set themselves up to fail. They literally create a realm that will bear out the accuracy of their destructive self-belief. Your convictions become self-fulfilling prophecies – as you believe, so are you.

There was a woman during the Great Depression who believed she would never have enough. The Depression provided very difficult years economically, and although she and her husband worked very hard, there was hardly enough to go around. The circumstances, year after year of the Depression, confirmed her mindset of lack. She developed a "core belief" that she would always experience deprivation – there would never be enough.

When the Great Depression ended, the family had a good income, yet she continued to believe there was not enough. She hoarded food, clothing, and other things. She over-purchased during sales and stored the excess in closets. She prepared very humble meals even though she could afford to feed her household better. She also stored money in various "secret places" around her home and had multiple bank accounts where she built up savings. Even with all of this, she never felt there was enough.

Before Christmas one year, her office manager invited each employee to donate fifty dollars to a fund to help the needy of the community. Her reply was, "I couldn't possibly give anything, as we can barely get by ourselves." She had carved out a *realm* of lack and withholding that she continually lived in, even though she had plenty. She never enjoyed abundance, because her beliefs had created fear. The world she lived in was a world of lack that she had created by her *beliefs*.

Truth Has to Be Made a Living Reality

Your core beliefs about God are extremely important. For example, if you really believe that God is always good, your belief will create a portal for God's goodness to manifest in your life. Scripture bears out that God's goodness and mercy endure forever (2 Chronicles 5:13). In addition, Psalm 23:6 teaches that God's goodness and mercy will follow you all the days of your life. God's intentions toward you are always good! If you believe that truth, then goodness will constantly be chasing you down. Your beliefs will carve out *realms* of goodness. Jesus said, "*Only* believe" (Mark 5:36, emphasis added).

We must re-train our minds to believe that God's Word is *the* Truth. You can believe something in a theoretical way yet not accept it as a reality by which you live. This is the difference between "belief" and "faith." You may believe in your mind that "God is love" and that He "loves you with an everlasting love." Should someone ask if you believe that God finds you loveable, you would immediately reply, "Yes," because it is established in your mind. However, if that truth is not formed in your heart (faith = an internal reality), then when rejected by your peers, you might believe that you are unlovable.

We need to meditate on truths about God until they become a living reality within us. When God's truth is truly established, it then becomes our default understanding about God, our world, and ourselves.

Establish the Word as the Truth You Live By

Your established, unshakable belief in the truth of God's Word is extremely important for creating an abundant, blessed life. When you align your core beliefs with God's truth, you establish your life in His divine desires for you.

I had a friend who read the Scriptures revealing Christ's commissioning for believers to preach the Good News of the Kingdom, heal the sick, raise the dead, cleanse lepers, and cast out demons (Matthew 10:7-8). He meditated on this word day and

We need to meditate on truths about God until they become a living reality within us.

night. He read related Scriptures repeatedly, engaged in times of soaking in those truths, dreamed about healing the sick, raising the dead, cleansing lepers, and casting out devils. He bought and read stacks of books written by famous healing evangelists and he built his faith daily. He acted on his belief and prayed for the sick at every opportunity. He would not allow anything to shake his faith; before long, he had carved out a miracle *realm* as a minister of the Gospel. Because he truly believed God's Word, masses of people were saved, healed, and set free. Believing in miracles, he created a *realm* of the miraculous and a worldwide miracle ministry.

Resist Lies – Believe Truth

One day, a friend shared during lunch that when her first-born child was about eighteen months old, someone in her church told her, "Oh, just wait until he turns two – there is nothing like the terrible twos! You'll see." The woman who shared that "ungodly wisdom" actually believed it; consequently, she had experienced it in her life. My friend decided then and there to resist that statement and refuse to believe it. Instead, she established a belief that all of her children would joyfully develop and none would go through the "terrible twos." She had four children and none of them did. She created a *realm* of blessing for her children, and when they turned two they were a joy to her. Her belief determined her outcome.

> Always believe what the Word says, and circumstances *must* eventually submit to a higher truth. Facts are temporal but truth is eternal.

Sometimes our circumstances are contrary to what we believe. My husband faced a health issue but our belief was that by the stripes of Jesus he was healed (confirmed in 1 Peter 2:24 KJV). Our belief stated one thing but circumstances communicated something else.

Always believe what the Word says, and circumstances *must* eventually submit to a higher truth. Facts are temporal (subject to time) but truth is eternal. Standing on the truth creates a *realm* for the manifestation of that truth within your *life*. Regardless of the adversity you face, if you continue to focus on the truth, the fact will eventually bow.

It might have been a fact that my husband had health issues, but the truth is he is a victor in Christ and has overcome.

A young man once shared with me his frustrations. His wife and child had been sick with flu and he prayed for them a number of times with all the faith he could muster. Yet, there was no evidence of a healing. He asked, "How long do I need to pray? It doesn't seem to be working!" I answered, "Pray until you have your breakthrough." Stand on the promise of healing until the manifestation comes.

The Devastating Effects of Unbelief

An *atmosphere* of faith is much more pleasant than an oppressive *atmosphere* of unbelief and fear. Honestly, I do not understand why some manifestations of the promises of God do not come immediately or, in some instances, on this side of eternity. However, I know one thing for certain: faith in God's promises creates an awesome *realm* on earth. It is always better to believe God's Word in circumstances contrary to His promises.

Israel created a *realm* of frustration for themselves while in the wilderness because of their unbelief in God's assurance of a Promised Land. Unbelief is not simply a lack of belief; it is actually believing something contrary. You only have two choices: believe in God's Word or the things that oppose it. Israel could have created heaven on earth with their faith and immediately entered their Promised Land. Instead, they spun their wheels for 40 years in the wilderness, and many of them never made it to their God-intended destination.

They believed that they were in a dry and dusty desert without their favorite food, "leeks and garlic," and that is exactly what they got. The entire time they traveled aimlessly and in discomfort, they could have had God's promise: a land flowing with olive oil and honey, a good land with fruit, water, wheat, a land without scarcity, with iron and copper, a land where they would lack for nothing (according to Deuteronomy 8:8-9). Their beliefs created their *realm* of life – a dusty desert. Oh, it could have been so different!

You cannot believe two conflicting things at the same time. You are either believing God's promises fully or you are not.

What Are Your Core Beliefs?

When I was turning sixty, I reevaluated and defined my core values and beliefs regarding God and myself. I took time to meditate on my fundamental beliefs.

The first one that came to my heart was, "God is Love."

I wrote down that core belief, pondered the various aspects of His love for days, and applied it to my daily life. I believe that God is love *all* the time. I believe everything He does is full of love and *He cannot act outside of love*. His gifts and even His disciplines are an expression of His love and He will never withdraw His love from me. These are important beliefs that form and shape my life. The more I meditate on His love, the more I am visited by it.

The next belief statement I wrote down was, "God is Good."

Again, I meditated on that for days, pondering the fullness of His goodness. I believe that "His goodness will follow me all the days of my life," and mercy endures forever. He will never hold back goodness from me. The more I pondered my beliefs about God's goodness, the more His goodness manifested.

The third statement was, "God is Righteous."

He always does the right thing. I can always trust Him because He never compromises. He is pure, holy, and full of integrity. I am safe with a righteous God. When I meditate on this truth and allow this belief to permeate me, I create a *realm* of righteousness in and through my life.

I continued developing my statement of twelve beliefs about God. Then I pasted them in my Bible and put them in my journal and various other places, to remind me continually of what I believe. I want these valued beliefs about God to be my "default" positions. I highly recommend that you also define what you *truly* believe about God.

What is Your Personal Mission Statement?

I created a new personal mission statement for my sixtieth year, containing twelve core beliefs about *who I am* and *why I live.*

My first statement is: I am a lover of Jesus and I live to bring Him pleasure.

This is who I am and why I live. When I remind myself of this, it gives me purpose and definition. When I arise in the morning, I refresh my belief in my purpose. Everything in my day is for Him because I love Him. I love Him because He first loved me. He is irresistible! I am a passionate lover of Jesus and all that I do is intended to bring Him pleasure. This gives my life purpose. My belief in who I am and why I live manifests in greater measure because I consciously define my beliefs.

My second statement is: I am a lover of people and I live to learn to love them more.

My greatest aim in life is to learn to love. When I remind myself of what I believe about myself, I grow in the manifestation of that belief and cause a *realm* of love for others to be created in "my world."

I also pasted my twelve personal mission statements in my Bible and review them often. I suggest that you prepare your own mission statement along with a statement of your core beliefs about God. It will define you and release you to create the world in which God intends for you to live.

Your beliefs create your world. What do you believe?

The Science of Believing

Dr. Aiko Hormann, a doctor of mathematics and physics, has practiced in her field since 1967. I met her when she was eighty-three years of age, and she was youthful, vibrant, and mentally sharp. She had been a scientist for forty-four years at the time we were introduced. As a scientist, she understands the functions of biophotons[7] and the biophoton fields found in and around the human body. The biophoton field is a created *realm* of light within the body that radiates beyond it and goes wherever we go.

She explained that each individual creates the essence of this field as their DNA molecules receive and transmit light frequencies. For example, if you are thinking negative thoughts and meditating on stressful things, the energy created in this field will have negative effects on your body and life. However, if you meditate on God's love, joy, and peace, and think on good things, the field of

---

[7]Source: Wikipedia. A biophoton (from the Greek βίος meaning "life" and φῶς meaning "light") is a photon of light emitted from a biological system and detected by biological probes as part of the general weak electromagnetic radiation of living biological cells. Biophotonics is the study, research, and application of photons in their interactions within and on biological systems. The typical detected magnitude of "biophotons" in the visible and ultraviolet spectrum ranges from a few, up to several hundred photons per second per square centimeter of surface area, much weaker than in the openly visible and well-researched phenomenon of normal bioluminescence, but stronger than in the thermal, or black body radiation that so-called perfect black bodies demonstrate. The detection of these photons has been made possible (and easier) by the development of more sensitive photomultiplier tubes and associated electronic equipment. Biophotons were employed by the Stalin regime to diagnose cancer, and their discoverer, Alexander Gurwitsch, was awarded the Stalin Prize. Various studies have indicated some potential for photon emission to be used as a diagnostic technique.

light produced will support health, favor with others, and strength in your body and life.

She further teaches that the scientific Law of Attraction[8] operates through the frequencies of the biophoton field. Consequently, if your mind is filled with negativity, fear, and stress, you create a negative field of energy within and around you that acts like a magnet attracting more negativity, fear, and stress. Science is confirming the Word of God.

Finally, brethren, whatever is true, whatever is honorable, whatever is right, whatever is pure, whatever is lovely, whatever is of good repute, if there is any excellence and if anything worthy of praise, dwell on these things (Philippians 4:8).

Your beliefs begin formation through the input you receive. If you sat under deceptive teachings day in and day out, you would begin to believe those things. It is important to submit yourself to Truth in order to establish godly beliefs. A person's behavior is always a manifestation of what they believe.

When you bask in the presence of the Lord, enjoying all He has given you, and when you delight in His liberating word of truth, you will manifest realms and atmospheres of grace and glory. Your beliefs will attract the substance of that which you believe.

If you, for example, believed legalistic and religious teachings, you would probably live in an atmosphere of self-condemnation, self-striving, guilt, and shame. You would be trapped in a world of oppression and bondage, and your soul would never feel free.

---

[8]Source: Wikipedia. In the history of science, the laws of attraction are a set of assumed laws or, in a sense, a general catch phrase used when discussing the nature of bodies that attract. Historically, the concept of there being a known set of the laws of attraction evolved from the laws of affinity, which numbered up to ten, depending upon which chemist was sourced.

However, if you gaze upon Christ's love for you and all that He accomplished for you on the Cross, the fear and striving will leave. Your whole being will be filled with liberty, joy, and freedom because the truth will set you free to live in an atmosphere of His divine bliss. Your world will then be filled with what you believe and You will attract more grace, more joy, and more liberty.

Take time to examine your core beliefs. Do you believe the truth about Christ's love for you? If not, make a change in what you believe – it is called repentance – simply turn away from false beliefs and snuggle up to Jesus and His love. And let the current of His outrageous love and amazing grace flow into you.

7

KEY #5—THE POWER TO CREATE THROUGH PRAISE AND THANKSGIVING

7

KEY #5—THE POWER TO CREATE THROUGH PRAISE AND THANKSGIVING

IN THIS CHAPTER WE FOCUS ON *PRAISE*, as we've already talked about *worship*. Many people use the words interchangeably, however they have two very different meanings. The definition I have found most helpful is by Ruth Ward Heflin: "We praise the Lord for all that He has done and for His mighty works, and we worship Him based on who He is." For example, I worship God for His love and I praise Him for how that love has affected my life through salvation and so much more. Neither is more important than the other. They both are essential to changing your *realms* and *atmospheres*.

A number of years ago, I listened to a CD teaching by my friend Joshua Mills on praise changing the atmosphere. Oh, it was so powerful! For days after hearing that teaching, I continued to proclaim: "Praise changes the *atmosphere*!"

The week prior to listening to Joshua's message had been particularly taxing, and discouragement was knocking at the door of my heart. Bombarded with one crisis after another, the temptation of self-pity and sadness visited me and attempted to take my focus off the victory promised in Christ. Then I began to act on what I had heard, and I praised the Lord. I praised … and praised …

and praised Him. Not only did all the discouragement and self-pity leave, but the praise stirred my faith, which created *realms* of breakthrough in many areas. In the coming days, I experienced great victories because of the praise. It was absolutely glorious!

Praise stirs up faith for breakthroughs.

The Sacrifice of Praise

When praising is the last thing you feel like doing, that is the time you need to do it the most, because it creates *realms* for God's goodness to manifest. I remember a time years ago when we were learning to live by faith, with no visible means of support. It was a challenging time for us as we stood on the Word of God without seeing immediate answers to His promises. We had to constantly keep our faith refreshed. I wish I could say that I walked blamelessly through that season, but there were times when I temporarily fell into whining and complaining. I am sharing this to encourage you, but my failures are so completely dissolved in the blood of His love it is as if I never failed even once. To move ahead, you have to see yourself as forgiven.

One day, during this period, I went to the fridge to get milk for my children's cereal, and the refrigerator was empty. As a result, I began to complain before God. In the middle of my murmuring, the Spirit of God reminded me of the murmuring of Israel in the wilderness, and I remembered that their murmuring didn't bring a positive outcome. The Lord invited me to praise Him instead of complaining. I began praising and thanking Him for all His goodness and for every blessing. I turned on the water faucet and praised Him that we had fresh water. I thanked Him for the dishes in the cupboard and for every item of food in the cupboards. I praised myself happy and my faith was restored.

Within twenty minutes of praising God, the doorbell rang. A woman I barely knew was standing there with a fresh gallon of milk that she had purchased at the farm up the street from us. She said a bit sheepishly, "I was buying my milk and thought the Lord told me to buy you some. Can you use it?" At the very time I started praising God, He opened a realm of provision. Oh, how good He is! Not only did we get milk but it was fresh from the cow!

Praise had released God's provision.

On the Mission Field [9]

Years ago, when I was on a mission field, I was put in charge of the kitchen and responsible for preparing three meals every day for about fifty people. When they gave me the position, the leadership informed me that I had a "faith budget." In other words, there was little in the *natural* to pay for the food – I had to *believe* for the food I cooked. They gave me a little money to cover a few of the essentials but it was not enough to purchase the food we needed.

Although I tried my best and attempted to be creative, I seemed to always be in trouble. We had a high carb–low protein diet because those were the cheapest foods available. The problem was, women get fat on carbs, and men get skinny due to the low protein. There were complaints about the food on a regular basis, and I felt terrible. The more I prayed and tried to cook nice meals, the more everyone complained, and the tighter the provisions became.

One day, while I was making bread and crying out to God: "Why am I not getting breakthrough in provision?" He answered, "It is because of the murmuring and complaining." He assured me that He had more than enough provisions but the negativity was hindering its release. We had actually made the heavens brass with

[9] Taken from *Help God, I'm Broke*

our complaining. I quickly shared with the others what the Lord revealed, and we had a time of repentance. Soon, the whole camp was praising and thanking God for every mouthful of food rather than grumbling. Within twenty-four hours of changing from complaining to praising, the miracles began! That is when Bessie the cow showed up – a gift from a local farmer. We had to learn how to milk her but from that day forward, we had loads of fresh milk, cream, and butter. It was wonderful.

However, that wasn't all! The next day, a local butcher began giving us fifteen kilos (over thirty pounds) of hamburger a week. This was a *major* blessing because we had very little meat in our diet, only a special chicken dinner once a month and the odd iguana that "Jungle Joe" (a young man in our school) shot for us. As you might guess, our team was not very fond of lizard meat, even though I tenderized it in a pressure cooker. So everyone was elated with the generous, weekly portion of beef.

In fact, food began coming in from every direction once we started praising and thanking the Lord for all things. Our breakthrough literally came overnight. Praise and thanksgiving had produced a *realm* of provision, miracles, and abundance.

Deliverance from Prison

Have you ever felt trapped, confined, or imprisoned by the situations in your life? Through praise, Paul and Silas created a miracle breakthrough from the chains that bound them:

The crowd rose up together against them, and the chief magistrates tore their robes off them and proceeded to order them to be beaten with rods. When they had struck them with many blows, they threw them into prison, commanding the jailer to guard them securely; and he, having received such a command, threw them into the inner prison and fastened their feet in the stocks. But about midnight Paul and Silas were *praying and singing hymns of praise* to God, and the prisoners were listening to them; and suddenly there came a great earthquake, so that the foundations of the prison house were shaken; and immediately all the doors were opened and everyone's chains were unfastened (Acts 16:22-26, emphasis added).

Their praise in the midst of that horrific treatment created a shift in the *atmosphere* and caused everything holding them in bondage to be shaken. Because of praise, they were set free. In addition, everyone in the prison was set free, AND the jailer along with his entire house was saved (Acts 16:27-32).

Praise can create *realms* of freedom for you, too. Things that have held you down and kept you from freedom will lose their power as you praise – and shifts will come.

You can praise your way into freedom.

Praise Until the Spirit of Worship Comes

In a book about glory written by Ruth Ward Heflin,[10] she made the following inspired statement:

> *Praise ... until the spirit of worship comes,*
> *Worship ... until the glory comes,*
> *Then ... stand in the glory!*

Her powerful book will fill you with faith as you read it. She explains that as we praise the Lord for all that He has done, worship will fill our hearts. Worship is based on who He is and not on what He does.

---

[10]Taken from *Glory: Experiencing the Atmosphere of Heaven* (MacDougal Press, 1990).

She encourages you to remember the mighty works the Lord has performed in your life and praise Him for them. She also exhorts the reader to praise Him for all the great works recorded in the Scripture.

As I read her book, I could not finish even a page without breaking into praise. Then a deep longing to worship would rise up in me, and soon the glory would come. The glory was often so thick that all I could do was bask in it.

Media Creates Atmospheres

Praise is the catalyst for worship and the visitation of the glory of the Lord. Start praising Him *now*.

We can use audio and video media to create *atmospheres*. I love to play praise and worship music in my study at home. It creates a holy *atmosphere* that you can actually feel. Put praise and worship music in every room of your home and office, if possible, and you will be amazed at the glory that falls. Sometimes I walk through my home releasing decrees of praise and thanksgiving, and my home and entire being becomes filled with glory. Praise brings God's presence on the scene: "You *are* holy, enthroned in the praises of [your people]" (Psalm 22:3 NKJV).

Praise is the catalyst for worship and the visitation of the glory of the Lord. Start praising Him *now* and you will see what I mean.

8

KEY #6—THE POWER OF THE SPOKEN WORD

8

Key #6—The Power of the Spoken Word

THE WORDS WE SPEAK ACTUALLY AFFECT OUR BODY and create the course of our life, as James declared:

> If anyone does not stumble in what he says, he is a perfect man, **able to bridle the whole body** as well. Now if we put the bits into the horses' mouths so that they will obey us, we direct their entire body as well. Look at the ships also, though they are so great and are driven by strong winds, are still directed by a very small rudder wherever the inclination of the pilot desires. So also **the tongue is a small part of the body, and *yet* it boasts of great things.** See how great a forest is set aflame by such a small fire! And the tongue is a fire, the *very* world of iniquity; **the tongue is set among our members as that which defiles the entire body, and sets on fire the course of *our* life.** (James 3:2-6, emphasis added).

According to Proverbs 18:21, "Death and life are in the power of the tongue, and those who love it will eat its fruit."

The words we speak create death or life; our words create *realms* and *atmospheres*. In the beginning, God created light through His words. He created order in the midst of chaos and substance within a void. All this came into being through His declared word:

> By faith we understand that the worlds were prepared by the word of God, so that what is seen was not made out of things which are visible (Hebrews 11:3).

The words you speak create your world. Choose your words carefully because they will either create a pathway of blessing or curse.

I once ministered in a region of America where you could actually feel an *atmosphere* of poverty, oppression, and fear. The precious Christians who attended the meeting were longing for a touch from God but it was evident that they had bought into the lie of oppression that prevailed over the area. The Lord gave me a word of knowledge for them: "Many of you are struggling financially and feel that there is never enough, and you have been speaking repeatedly, 'I can't afford it' and 'I don't have enough.'"

Continuing to exhort them in the Lord, I asked anyone who identified with that word to come to the altar for prayer. Almost everyone in the room came forward. They had been under the oppression of spirits of lack and poverty of that region, and their confessions fed those demonic spirits. Every time they confessed lack, they empowered demons of lack. It created a growing realm of want in the region that affected the entire community.

Then I encouraged those at the altar to repent and receive forgiveness for speaking contrary to the Word of God that declares plenty. They needed to wipe their slate clean and begin sowing words that would bring blessing to their lives and a positive effect in their *realms* of influence. Up to that time, the meeting had felt heavy but when they repented and started proclaiming the blessings, there was a notable atmospheric shift in the room. Joy and faith permeated the sanctuary, and from there it could spread to influence the community.

Speak Life-Giving Words

Jesus said this about His words: "The words that I have spoken to you are spirit and are life" (John 6:63).

Early in my Christian walk, I learned the power of decreeing the Scriptures. I found amazing verses in the Bible promising blessing for my life. I wrote them on a sheet of paper and then proclaimed the promises in faith with an intentional focus. I discovered that the proclamation of the Word of God was powerful and brought breakthroughs and goodness in my life. I actually wrote a book called *Decree*, full of proclamations of the Word for various areas of your life. There are decrees for victory, wisdom, blessing, glory, favor, family, health, business, finance, and many other areas of your life. It takes approximately one hour to proclaim all the decrees in the book. When I have the opportunity, I proclaim the decrees a number of times throughout the day, and I often experience a shift occurring in my heart and mind. Following a recitation of the decrees, I also notice goodness and blessing manifesting in areas of my life.

"Decree a thing and it will be established for you" (Job 22:28).

This is a powerful promise: "Decree a thing, and it will be established for you" (Job 22:28).

Decree is a legal term that often speaks of "a final decision or judgment in a court of law." The dictionary definition[11] is:

---

[11] Webster's Online Dictionary

1. An official order

2. A court ruling

3. A divine order

4. To issue an order for something to happen

God's promises are decrees made in the court of heaven over your life. In Esther 8:8, the Scripture states that a decree made in the name of the king will not be revoked. King Jesus is the King of kings, and it is very powerful when we make decrees of His Word in His name.

God says in Isaiah 55:11 that His Word will not return void but will accomplish everything it is sent to do. When you decree God's Word over your life daily, the manifestation of that Word will come upon your life.

Decree the Word of God to create realms of His blessing.

Another powerful way to create an *atmosphere* of truth and faith is to play audio files of the Scriptures in your home, study, car, or workplace. The authority of the Word will release the essence of its truth in your *sphere*. The more we fill the earth with the Word of God, the more we will see the world come into alignment with it.

Move that Mountain!

Let's study these powerful words of Jesus!

Truly, I say to you, **whoever says to this mountain**, "Be taken up and cast into the sea," and does not doubt in his heart, **but believes that what he says is going to happen**, it will be *granted* him (Mark 11:23, emphasis added).

In this passage, Jesus is clearly teaching about the power of words that you declare with pure faith and authority against the "mountains" in your life. Mountains can be obstacles. What obstacles are in your way? Some would answer – the mountain of debt, an impossible relational situation, a health challenge, or even extra body weight. Note that Jesus did not instruct us to *talk about* the mountain, He said, "*Speak* to it!"

In your prayer times, begin to declare the removal of your personal mountain. Do not be discouraged if it does not move immediately, but continue decreeing *until* it does move. That is how we paid off a mortgage on a home. We began to apply declaration of being debt-free every day to the loan on our home, and within nine months, the mortgage was gone. Be tenacious and do not move off your decree until the mountain moves.

Victory Over Depression

A woman I knew struggled with depression and didn't even want to get out of bed in the morning. When she did get up, she moped about all day long. Her worldview was extremely negative and, as a result, her home felt oppressed. She had created an *atmosphere* of heaviness.

When I visited her one day, she explained that she had no desire to face life any more. She didn't want to get out of bed most days and felt overcome by depression. I gave her decrees to proclaim over her life. They were Scriptures that stated she was the head and not the tail, above and not beneath, and that she was an overcomer in this life. I gave her a whole page of decrees. At first she did not want to even bother reading them, but I persisted. I sat beside her and made her proclaim them. Her first effort was very weak so I made her read them again.

I had done this exercise with a family member years before and had great success. That gave me confidence to press in even though she was resisting. She read them once more but again without enthusiasm. After the second reading, she thanked me and then politely asked me to leave. However, I persisted and said, "Read them a third time, and this time, really mean what you are saying."

With hesitation, she did as I asked and we had the first glimmer of a breakthrough. She sounded a *little* encouraged after that time so we went for a fourth reading. Every time she read the declarations, her countenance brightened a bit, and she realized that the Word was actually having affect. I left her with the decrees and instructed her to continue to proclaim them over and over. She followed through and every day she experienced more breakthrough until a day came that she made it all the way out of her depression. The Word delivered her; the decrees created a realm of victory in her life and brightened the *atmosphere* of her home. There was a definite shift!

Decrees of God's Word have creative power because God's Word is the final authority. The words you speak actually are important. They create life or death – blessing or curse. The words you speak create *your world!*

When you stand in faith on God's Word, and proclaim it over yourself and your situations, you create *realms* of life and blessings.

> When you stand in faith on God's Word and proclaim it over yourself and your situations, you create *realms* of life and blessings.

9

KEY #7—THE POWER TO CREATE THROUGH SOWING AND REAPING

9

KEY #7—THE POWER TO CREATE THROUGH SOWING AND REAPING

Sowing[12]

IF YOU WANT ABUNDANCE, THEN SOW according to what the Word teaches. I have watched it work for many years in every area of my life. God made a perpetual promise in Genesis 8:22 when He declared, "While the earth remains, seedtime and harvest … shall not cease." Since the earth still remains, this promise is in effect today. If you sow a seed, there *will be* a corresponding harvest; it is both a natural and a spiritual law.

The principle of sowing and reaping is easy to grasp. If I plant bean seeds in a natural garden, I will grow beans (not corn). Regardless of how many bean seeds I plant, I will reap *more* beans than I planted. The more beans I plant the better the harvest. If I sow my seeds into good, rich soil, I will reap more bountifully. When I plant my seed and it grows to a full plant, it contains seeds inside the fruit it produces.

---

[12]Portions of this chapter are taken from *Help God, I'm Broke* (Patricia King, XP Publishing, 2010).

You create *realms* and *atmospheres* through sowing and reaping in the same way a farmer creates a harvest. For example, if you desire to become a successful brain surgeon, you need to sow into your dream. You would sow education, study, finances, discipline, internship, and perseverance until you reap the reward of your doctorate degree as a neurosurgeon. You would never be allowed to operate on anyone's brain without sowing into the process.

If you long for a healthy, slim and trim body, then you would not want to sow into your body a diet of chocolate bars, rich desserts, fast foods, unhealthy fats, along with lack of exercise and sleep. No, no! Those are the seeds you would sow if you wanted to reap an overweight body subject to diabetes and heart disease. To live in a realm of health and fitness, you will have to sow into it.

The same principle works with relationships. For example, if you desire a strong, healthy, loving marriage, you need to sow good seed into your marriage. If you and your spouse sow prayer, unconditional love, forgiveness, faithfulness, uplifting communication and actions, patience, and unwavering sacrifice and commitment, you will reap a strong marriage. A healthy *atmosphere* in the realm of marriage is dependent on what you sow.

Soil Is Significant

The nature of the soil you sow into is important. I always look for soil that is conducive to productivity and Kingdom advancement. If you sow finances into good soil, you will receive an abundant harvest in your finances. For example, if you intend to invest financially into a business, you would look for an industry that can bring a good return. You would not invest into a company owned by a drug addict who is millions of dollars in debt and lacking in integrity. That is not good soil. You should look for businesses or ministries to sow into that are rich in faith, love, and character.

You can sow your way into realms of prosperity and abundance, and even sow your way out of debt. I speak from experience because I have lived by this Kingdom principle for more than thirty-five years in my personal life, businesses, and ministries!

Our ministry needed to build a new studio. It was approximately a million dollar project. When we were about to move forward, God put it in our heart to build a home for abused children in Asia. We were so touched by the need that we decided to sow into the children's home rather than raise funds for our own building. I told the missionary that we would build the home for him. We needed one hundred thousand dollars to cover the building cost and the care of the children for the first year. God blessed as we raised the funds, and we were able to give them the entire amount. As a result, we have rescued more than thirty children from being child soldiers in Asia. Now they are safe and loved.

After that, we wanted to proceed with our project, but another need came up. This time a friend of ours was trying to purchase a building in Cambodia that could house girls coming out of the sex trade, so we raised another one hundred thousand dollars for that need. Then, a family on our team felt led to move to Africa to help orphans. They needed to raise sixty thousand dollars to cover their move, so we committed to sowing into them and covering that need.

Every time we wanted to move forward to raise funds for our television studio, another pressing need came to our attention. Our team in Thailand felt an urgent need to start a shelter for children coming out of the sex trade, and so we committed to that need and met it. At the same time, many of our ministry friends were engaged in building projects, so we sowed something into everyone who asked.

Finally, the Lord gave us the go-ahead to raise finances for a new studio that would create Christian media to be broadcast all over the world. We had nothing to start with because we had sown and sown and sown our precious seed into good soil. However, when you add it all up and multiply it by one hundredfold, we could expect a large return – the harvest would be more than what we needed. With absolute confidence, we moved forward with our building and stood in faith, calling forth the return on the seed we had sown into all those building projects. As a result, all of our needs for the building were met and we were able to pay cash for everything.

Not only were we able to complete our building debt free, but the Lord also gave us the blessing of starting an outreach center in Cambodia with all its expenses met. By sowing into mission and ministry buildings, we created a realm of blessing in "buildings" and fruitful mission projects. The result was beyond anything we could have dreamed. God is so very faithful to fulfill His Word!

This is how dreams become realities – sow with purpose and intention to receive your return.

Seed to Scatter

To obtain a harvest, you need seed to sow. The Scriptures teach that God furnishes seed to the sower and will even multiply your seed for sowing:

Now He who supplies seed to the sower and bread for food will supply and multiply your seed for sowing and increase the harvest of your righteousness (2 Corinthians 9:10).

If you truly want to sow but don't have seed, then simply ask the Lord for seed to sow. He will give it to you. Sometimes people say, "Oh, if only I had some money, I would care for the poor." Well, ask for the seed to sow and if you really want to help the poor, God will give you the seed to do so. He has never failed me yet when I have asked Him for seed.

Just remember not to eat your seed. If you eat your seed for sowing by using it to fulfill your desires, then there is none left to sow and create your harvest. If you ask for seed and it comes into your hand, then sow it – do not spend it. When you sow your seed, it will not only produce bread for you to eat, it will provide more seed for sowing.

One of the ways I have helped people get out of poverty is to give them not only help for their immediate need but also seed to sow. I always emphasize: ***Do not spend this seed! Sow it!*** I know that if they sow in faith, according to the Word of God, they will enjoy an increase. Then, if they give from their increase, they will reap even more.

This is how dreams become realities – sow with purpose and intention to receive your return.

I met a young woman once who was trapped in rejection and self-pity. Since early childhood, she had experienced a very difficult upbringing in a series of foster homes. She had a "love deficit." She felt lonely and rejected at school and had no friends but desperately wanted to belong. I listened with compassion as she shared her heart, but my compassion alone could not change her situation. I encouraged her to sow love into the lives of others. She lacked love and had never really experienced love, but I assured her that God would give her what she lacked. I encouraged her to become a volunteer for a ministry at our church that visited the elderly at a nursing home. The next Sunday after church, I accompanied her on the outreach. We prayed before we left and asked the Lord to give her love to sow into the lonely elderly people she would meet that day.

The outreach was a success and she learned to care for and love the elderly, and joined the outreach every week after that. As she sowed love and friendship into the lives of the elderly, she began to reap in other areas as well. She became friends with one of the girls on the outreach team and things in her life began to change. She was reaping a realm of meaningful relationships in her life because she sowed a seed of love. Initially, she did not have the seed to sow to reap her desired harvest, so she asked God. He will always give you your seed to sow.

Intentional Harvesting Is Important

Many have grasped the principle of sowing and they are faithful sowers. *Intentional reaping*, however, is also vital to create your desired realm. What would you think of a farmer who loved to sow but was shy about reaping or perhaps even resistant to it? He joyfully and abundantly threw his seed out into a field saying, "Yippee, I *love* sowing! I don't care about the reaping. I just love to sow! Yippee!" If you were an onlooker, you would think he was an absolute lunatic.

Here is another scenario: a farmer faithfully sowed seed into his field. It is good ground and the seed produces him an abundant harvest. But harvest time comes and goes and when you drive by weekly, you watch the neglected harvest rot and die. One day you meet the farmer while shopping in town and ask him why he didn't reap the field. "Oh," he says, "if God wants me to have a harvest, He will give me one. I am just going to be a faithful sower."

That makes *no* sense. God gave him the harvest, it was right in front of his eyes every day, but he failed to put the sickle in the ground and reap. It is the same in the spirit realm; you sow by faith *but* you must also *intentionally reap by faith*. Many Christians are faithful in sowing but are not aware of reaping. Some are actually resistant to reaping, because they believe it is ungodly to desire a harvest.

I have actually heard people make comments like the farmer in the story above. They say things like, "If God wants me to have a return on my sowing, He will give it," or "I love sowing and sacrificing, but I don't care if I get a return." These responses make no sense and they will definitely not bring forth the fruit of abundance. A farmer sows with the intention to reap and so should you. When you sow faithfully into good ground, a harvest awaits you. Believe for your desired realm to manifest and call it forth in faith with intention and focus.

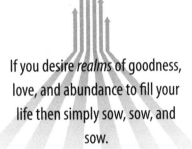

If you desire *realms* of goodness, love, and abundance to fill your life then simply sow, sow, and sow.

Reap in the Time of Harvest

Some people get discouraged when they sow one day and don't reap the next. There is a time for sowing and a time for reaping. You have to let your seed grow. I have found that some of the seed I sowed almost twenty years ago is still bearing fruit today, like perennials. Some seeds produce a quick harvest while others take time; it is the same in the natural. Some vegetables, like Swiss chard, produce a quick harvest in a few weeks, but an apple tree takes a few years.

Be patient and wait for your harvest. Don't dig up your seed every day to see if it is producing. It will! In 2 Corinthians 9:6-11 we read:

Now this I say, he who sows sparingly will also reap sparingly, and he who sows bountifully will also reap bountifully. Each one must do just as he has purposed in his heart, not grudgingly or under compulsion, for God loves a cheerful giver. And God is able to make all grace abound to you, so that always having all sufficiency in everything, you may have an abundance for every good deed; as it is written, "HE SCATTERED ABROAD, HE GAVE TO THE POOR, HIS RIGHTEOUSNESS ENDURES FOREVER." Now He who supplies seed to the sower and bread for food will supply and multiply your seed for sowing and increase the harvest of your righteousness; you will be enriched in everything for all liberality, which through us is producing thanksgiving to God (emphasis added).

The Garden of Life

One day I gave my grandson a little illustrated life lesson that I called "Planting Your Garden of Life." I explained to him that whatever he desired in life, he needed to sow a seed for the outcome in the same way that we would plant a vegetable garden. I taught him the principles of sowing and reaping, and exhorted him to sow only what he wanted to reap because he would always reap more than he sowed. He drew a picture of a beautiful garden and made rows of things he desired to grow. We then discussed what seeds would produce his desired harvest. He loved the lesson. This is a simple illustration but valuable for everyone.

If you desire *realms* of goodness, love, and abundance to fill your life, then simply sow, sow, and sow. Eventually, you will harvest a bountiful crop ... and oh, take care of the weeds along the way! You will definitely want a crop failure on those "weed seeds"!

10

Key #8—The Power to Create Through the Tithe

10

Key #8—The Power to Create Through the Tithe

The First and the Best Goes to God![13]

SCRIPTURAL TEACHING ON THE TITHE REFERS TO FINANCES. I realize that. But I have discovered that *realms* of blessing open up over my life whenever I offer God the first and the best of everything. At the end of this chapter I will share a testimony regarding the tithing of time.

Tithing for New Testament Believers

The tithe, which means ten percent, belongs to the Lord. Genesis 14:18-20, records when the tithe was first offered by Abraham to Melchizedek, king of Salem and "priest of God Most High." God was delighted in this act and blessed Abraham as a result. Later, this act was made law so that all of Israel could live in the same blessing as Abraham.

In the New Testament, however, we are not under the law and we don't tithe out of duty; instead, we offer the tithe through the

---

[13]Portions of this chapter are taken from *Help God, I'm Broke*

Kingdom's love law. Rather than fulfilling a *law*, we give to show our *love* and to affirm our sonship; the tithe is an expression of heartfelt worship by grateful sons and daughters. The blessings of the tithe then come upon us just as they did for tithers under the old covenant. Malachi 3:10-12 says:

> Bring the whole tithe into the storehouse, so that there may be food in My house, and test Me now in this," says the Lord of hosts, "if I will not open for you the windows of heaven and pour out for you a blessing until it overflows. Then I will rebuke the devourer for you, so that it will not destroy the fruits of the ground; nor will your vine in the field cast its grapes," says the Lord of hosts. "All the nations will call you blessed, for you shall be a delightful land," says the Lord of hosts.

Look at the *realms of blessings* you are promised because of tithing:

1. He will open the heavens over your life.
2. He will pour out a blessing that you will not have room to contain.
3. He will rebuke the devourer on your behalf.
4. Your fruitfulness will not be lost.
5. The nations will call you blessed.
6. You will be a delightful land.

From the time I was saved, I tithed. Immediately after receiving Christ, I had the desire to give Him my all and I have never skipped tithing for more than thirty-five years. This is because I quickly learned the value of bringing the tithe. When you tithe you are saying, "God, You are more important to me than anything else in life!" In Malachi, we are taught that the tithe belongs to the Lord, and

He actually rebuked Israel when they withheld it. He said they were robbing Him by neglecting tithes and offerings (Malachi 3:8-9).

Can I Afford It?

I have heard many say that they cannot afford to tithe when finances are tight. I personally believe that we can't afford *not* to tithe if we are in a hard place. I would rather give the Lord what belongs to Him and do without myself. "Where your treasure is, there your heart will be also," or to rephrase Luke 12:34 in modern language, "What you do with your money shows who or what has captured your heart."

> If our hearts belong to Christ, then even in the most difficult times, we should give Him the first and best – it belongs to Him.

If our hearts belong to Christ, then even in the most difficult times, we should give Him the first and best – it belongs to Him.

Consider this scenario: an investor came into partnership with a bankrupt individual who had no money to invest and no assets. The investor said, "I will give all that I have into this investment, and all I want is the first ten percent return on the gross. You can have the remaining ninety percent and manage the account." What a glorious partnership for the bankrupt individual. He was obviously happy about that arrangement, as anyone would be. He made no investment, had a promise of success, and received ninety percent of the gross profit. On the other hand, the investor gave everything into the investment.

When it was time for the individual to set aside the investor's ten percent one month, he decided he could not fulfill his obligation.

He had used his ninety percent to repair his vehicle, pay the rent and utilities, buy some new clothes, purchase items online, and pay off some bills. After that, although he was a little short for the rest of the month, he took his family out for a movie and pizza, and bought an advanced satellite package for his television. After all, he deserved to have a bit of pleasure because he worked hard and had done without in the past! He thought he would wait until the next month and catch up, but a similar scenario developed the following month and for each subsequent month. He got used to spending the investor's money each month.

After a year, the investor asked for his ten percent. The individual explained that he was sorry but he could not afford to pay what he owed. Let me ask you, "What would you do if you were the investor?" Not only is withholding the ten percent illegal, actually embezzlement, but it is selfish and foolish. He had the perfect business partner, a dream-come-true, and he blew it!

In my parable, Jesus is like the investor. He gave His entire life – all He is and all He has. We are like the bankrupt individual who received Jesus' gift of life, Kingdom power and authority, while dead in trespasses and sin.

My life is no longer my own; it belongs to Him.

I have heard people say, "Yes, but it is *my* money because *I* worked for it." If that is your take on it, then you have not understood your salvation. When we come to Christ, there is an exchange – He gives you His life and you give Him yours. All that He is and has, becomes yours; all that you were, are, and have becomes His.

My life is no longer my own; it belongs to Him. "For if we live, we live to the Lord; and if we die, we die to the Lord. Therefore, **whether we live or die, we are the Lord's**" (Romans 14:8 NKJV, emphasis added).

Tithing establishes that truth because it demonstrates that I realize my life fully belongs to Him. What an awesome blessing that He only asks for ten percent. Investors in the world would never offer that kind of deal. They would never give you something for nothing, let alone offer you ninety percent of a blessed income.

God does not need your money. However, *you need His partnership.*

Most governments ask for much more than ten percent of your income in taxes and do not give anywhere near as much in return. Yet the King of all kings in whose Kingdom you are a citizen asks only for ten percent. The reason the Lord requests the first ten percent is to engage you in the fullness of His blessings.

God does not need your money. However, *you need His partnership* so that all the finances remaining in your hand are touched by blessing. The same power of blessing and multiplication that Jesus released to feed a multitude from a boy's lunch is released over the remaining ninety percent.

During our testing season in personal finances, we never withheld the tithe. I remember saying to God one day that I would rather do without *everything* than withhold *anything* due Him. It was truly a difficult season for a while, even though we were faithful in our tithes. However, after a few years, the blessings began coming in on every wave, and they still do.

That test revealed what was in our hearts. We discovered through the trials that our love for God was stronger than *anything* money could buy. I believe the prosperity we enjoy today is based on our faithfulness in tithing. **Tithing is one of the most powerful expressions of worship.** Over the years, we increased our faith to tithe more and more. We went from one tithe to two tithes, then three, and we continue to increase it. I love tithing and its benefits!

Tithing Your Time

As a ministry, we have always put a lot of emphasis on prayer. I believe that any failure in ministry or in life is first a failure in prayer.

The more we prayed as a ministry, the more fruitful we became, and that fruit demanded more of our attention. As a result, we began compromising corporate prayer time in order to accomplish all the work assignments.

Through the tithe, you create a *realm* of open heaven, victory, increase, and Kingdom abundance over your life.

One day, the Lord strongly convicted me concerning this, so we set a policy that our workday would begin with one hour of corporate prayer. We took the first hour out of eight (more than a tithe) to give to the Lord in worship and prayer. This was in addition to our own private devotion time. Immediately we noticed the blessing. We were able to accomplish more work in less time when we gave Him the first and the best. An open heaven prevailed in every department of the ministry when we made this adjustment.

Through the tithe, you create a *realm* of open heaven, victory, increase, and Kingdom abundance over your life.

11

Key #9—The Power to Create Through Focus and Passion

11

KEY #9—THE POWER TO CREATE THROUGH FOCUS AND PASSION

*Whatever you focus on, ultimately,
you will empower in your life:*

*Negative Focus Creates Negative Realms,
Positive Focus Creates Positive Realms*

What you focus on creates influences, profound and powerful, even in your physical body. Science can actually measure the light frequencies (energy fields) your body creates. They have found that these fields intensify or diminish based on whether your focus is positive or negative.

For example, if you are focused on the "fear of lack," which results in not having enough money to pay your bills, then the fear you are focused on creates energy frequencies within your body that can negatively affect both your peace and your health. This measurable tension within the body can create an environment for producing sickness and disease. In addition, the spiritual power generated by believing in your fears can actually bring the manifestation of that which you fear. It happened to Job, "For the thing I greatly feared has come upon me, and what I dreaded has happened to me" (Job 3:25 NKJV).

On the other hand, if you focus on the creative and positive, it will give you joy. Your *focus* can also cause a release of hormones and chemicals that bring health, strength, and harmony in the body and soul. In addition, it makes possible the release of creative energy to manifest fruitfulness in your life.

Perhaps this is why Paul taught the church at Philippi to:

Rejoice in the Lord always; again I will say, rejoice! Let your *gentle* spirit be known to all men. The Lord is near. Be anxious for nothing, but in everything by prayer and supplication with thanksgiving let your requests be made known to God. And the peace of God, which surpasses all comprehension, will guard your hearts and your minds in Christ Jesus. Finally, brethren, whatever is true, whatever is honorable, whatever is right, whatever is pure, whatever is lovely, whatever is of good repute, if there is any excellence and if anything worthy of praise, dwell on these things (Philippians 4:4-8, emphasis added).

The Color of Cancer

The doctor of a friend of mine who was fighting cancer instructed her to avoid focusing on the cancer and the fear it creates. He told her to focus *only* on the positive and hopeful things in her life, especially those things that make her happy and create laughter. He explained that the deliberate intention to focus on the positive had the potential to release chemicals that would help her body heal. Her positive focus could actually create a realm of health and strength, and cancer cells could not survive in that *atmosphere*. He also stated that laughter truly works as a healer:

A cheerful heart is good medicine, but a broken spirit saps a person's strength (Proverbs 17:22 NLT).

Negative thoughts create the opposite – a *realm* and *atmosphere* for sickness and disease to flourish. In other words, what we focus on can determine the realm of health in our body.

Physicists have developed sophisticated equipment that measures light frequencies and their associated colors. This equipment can determine the effect that negative and positive words and emotions have on our bodies. They have even invented tools capable of scanning the body from head to toe to determine the presence of disease by reading the light frequencies and colors our bodies emit. Through this diagnostic testing, they can also isolate where the problems are centered and the intensity of the disease or infirmity. A physicist told me that bright purples and blues reveal vibrant health, while the lower colors on the light spectrum indicate ill health.

Whatever You Focus On, You Create

Focus controls the creation of the *realms* and *atmospheres* that create your world. I once had a deadline to finish a book for our publisher and I was far from completing it. Many distractions kept arising, so I booked a hotel room for two days to help me stay focused and complete the assignment. I checked into the room, turned on my computer, and worked on the assignment until it was completed.

Although I did not answer my cell phone or read my emails, at first my mind was distracted with many thoughts and I could not concentrate on the book. So, I prayed, cast down thoughts that did not pertain to writing the book, and brought my thoughts into focus on the project. Before long, I was on a roll and able to finish the book in record time. Focus, concentrating solely on the project, created the completion of the assignment.

Creating Realms of Successful Kingdom Ministry

As a young Christian, I loved soul winning because I longed for others to enjoy the same forgiveness, freedom, and new life that I had received in Christ. As a result, I stayed up late at night thinking of ways to win souls. I was focused! Then when I awoke the next day, I would implement those ideas on the streets. I spent hours praying for souls each day. Then when I went out witnessing, I always won someone to the Lord, because my focus created the fruit of that upon which I had focused.

Day after day, month after month, and year after year, I focused on winning souls. In time, I began seeing an increase in the number of souls coming into the Kingdom. My fruit was increasing. In fact, I was creating a "realm of salvation." One night I answered the door and a man was standing there. When I asked if I could help him, he replied, "I need to get saved, can you help me?" Another time, I was at our church with a couple of friends, praying for souls, and a man walking down the street came into the church and asked us if we could introduce him to Jesus. Another time, I received a phone call at 2 a.m. from someone I worked with who asked if I could help them come to know God. I was no longer simply following my focus, but the fruit of my focus was actually following me.

Eventually, I was asked to teach and train others in personal evangelism. My focus on soul winning produced an expanded realm that was imparted to others. The Lord then called me to television media where we reach the masses with the gospel of Christ. The realm has continued to expand.

However, I found that when I became busy with other aspects of ministry that required focus and time commitments, the intense soul winning focus shifted. As my focus weakened, so also did my deliberate actions of soul winning; as a result, the fruit became less even though souls were still being reached. There is a correlation between your focus and your fruit.

A friend of mine who is a very anointed musician, songwriter, and worship leader focused on music from an early age and learned to play many instruments. Everything in his life has been related to music, song writing, and worship. He lives in a constant realm of worship and seldom has to search out new songs; the inspiration for new songs comes spontaneously. He carved out and established a fruitful realm of worship through intense focus.

Passion's Power

In the preceding examples, passion was the key to the intense focus that produced *realms* of fruitfulness. I find it easy to focus if I am passionate about something. I find it difficult to focus if I am not (although shear willpower and determination will enable you to focus whether you have passion or not). Passion is truly a great motivator.

As a leader, I love to discover what my team members are most passionate about. If I can place them in a position where their passion is ignited, they are usually exceedingly focused and fruitful!

Passion and focus will carve out *your* realm of success as you discover and acknowledge *your* God-given gifts and pursue them with passion.

Athletes know the power of passion and focus. When speaking with a sports trainer on an airplane one day, I asked him what he believed was the greatest factor for success in athletics. He replied that it is undoubtedly the individual's passion. He explained that he had met many gifted individuals but they always fell short of their potential if they lacked passion. Lacking passion, they failed to focus on practice and their game.

He further explained that he would rather work with a passionate athlete than a gifted one who lacked passion, because the passionate athlete could develop the skills and breakthrough into a realm of excellence with enough focus and perseverance. He emphasized that the very best case scenario is to find an individual who was both gifted and filled with passion and focus.

Passion and focus will carve out *your* realm of success as you discover and acknowledge *your* God-given gifts and pursue them with passion.

While on a cruise holiday with our family, we really enjoyed one of the entertainers in the evening shows. He had all the children in awe and laughter. At the end of his performance, he explained that he had practiced entertaining since childhood. He had a passion for the stage, loved to make people laugh and, as a result, took training to mature his talents. He diligently practiced and took every opportunity to entertain family and friends. His passion and focus produced a gifted, favored, and successful career that, as an adult, took him all around the world.

Passion and Focus Release the Miracle Realm

Look at what Scripture says about Elijah's passionate and focused prayers:

Elijah was a man with a nature like ours, and he prayed earnestly that it would not rain, and it did not rain in the earth for three years and six months. Then he prayed again, and the sky poured rain and the earth produced its fruit (James 5:17-18).

Through passion and focus, Elijah created effectual prayers that started and then ended a drought in the land, releasing a realm of blessing for the nation. "The effectual fervent prayer of a righteous man availeth much" (James 5:16 KJV).

I have discovered that intensely passionate, focused, and targeted prayer produces what is prayed for. On the other hand, I have discovered that passionless prayer seldom produces results. Prayers that lack passion are without a creative force behind them.

Years ago, I worked with a man of God in Nigeria who was one of the most faith-filled individuals I ever met. He lived in a region that was once known as a realm of gross wickedness due to its domination by satanism. When the Lord directed him to start a ministry in the region, he immediately began with a forty-day fast of only water.

He prayed day and night, hour by hour, to prepare his heart to overcome the wickedness in his region. His undying focus became the Word

Perhaps we could say the passionate, focused prayer of a righteous man avails much.

of God and its authority to overpower the enemy. In the years following, he built a realm of light and testimony for the glory of God in that region. Satanism had to bow to the gospel because this man created a realm of Kingdom authority that prevailed over the darkness. His secret to success was his passion and focus.

Mother Theresa will always be known for her success in helping the poor, oppressed, and dying. She lived a life of devotion, focused on those God called her to help. As a result, she carved out a realm of authority that brought her before leaders of governments, commerce, and religion. Her words and actions live on after her death. The *realms* we create are not confined to our lifetime, the fruit of our created *realms* lives on.

Focus is a powerful key to creating YOUR WORLD!

12

Key #10—The Power to Create Through Action and Aesthetics

12

Key #10—The Power to Create Through Action and Aesthetics

The Power of Action

Scripture teaches that faith without works is dead (James 2:17). Your actions definitely create *realms* and *atmospheres*. For example, let's say that you want to lose weight. You prayed and asked God to help you, and you believe that He will, but right after prayer you went out to have pizza, followed by many trips to the chocolate dessert buffet. The next morning you intended to go to the gym but put it off so you could sleep in. That evening, instead of going to the gym, you sat on the couch and watched a movie.

In this scenario, your actions are violating your desire. If you desire to live in the realm of vibrant health, then you need to adjust your actions ... eat nutritious, low calorie meals and regularly go to the gym. The actions of eating bad food followed by "couch-potato ministry" *will* produce a realm, but not the one you desire. To be trim and healthy, you have to carry out the corresponding actions.

Knock on Lots of Doors

A missionary at our church shared his story about how he became successful as a missionary. He explained that he began as a door-to-door salesman selling hair products as a teenager. In his sales training, he learned that the key to success in selling his product was "knocking on lots of doors." Every day he would knock on as many doors as he could. He knew that the more homes he visited, the more possibilities he would have to sell his product. With this one key and much determination and focus, he became a very successful salesman in his company in a short time.

Years later, he went to India as a missionary and he used the same principle when he went into villages where the gospel had never been preached. He knew that by knocking on lots of doors he would have more opportunities to reach people for Christ. His actions produced results.

In his first year as a missionary, he knocked on thousands of doors and preached the gospel to everyone who would listen. It took months of persistent, unrelenting action to get his first convert. Then he won more and more people to the Lord, and during his years of service in India he planted hundreds of churches, started Bible schools, and raised up many leaders. The realm of the Kingdom of God came to India through his actions and service. His realm of success as a missionary was due to his deliberate actions, not merely his desires or prayers.

Put actions to your dreams and create realms
and atmospheres.

I know many people who have awesome dreams and desires, yet lack a plan of action to bring their dreams to pass. Your dreams require action. My father used to quote a saying that stuck in my mind: *"Whatever you vividly imagine, ardently desire, and enthusiastically act upon will inevitably come to pass."* —Paul J. Meyers

Activate Your Talents

God's goodness will fill your *realms* of influence as you activate your God-given authority to rule and your power to create. In addition, your world will increase and multiply with blessings as you faithfully steward your current *realms*. When you are faithful in little, God will give you more.

Jesus shared a parable that explains this Kingdom principle:

"For *it is* just like a man *about* to go on a journey, who called his own slaves and entrusted his possessions to them. To one he gave five talents, to another, two, and to another, one, each according to his own ability; and he went on his journey. Immediately the one who had received the five talents went and traded with them, and gained five more talents. In the same manner the one who had received the two *talents* gained two more. But he who received the one *talent* went away, and dug *a hole* in the ground and hid his master's money.

"Now after a long time the master of those slaves came and settled accounts with them. The one who had received the five talents came up and brought five more talents, saying, 'Master, you entrusted five talents to me. See, I have gained five more talents.' His master said to him, 'Well done, good and faithful slave. You were faithful with a few things, I will put you in charge of many things; enter into the joy of your master.'

"Also the one who *had received* the two talents came up and said, 'Master, you entrusted two talents to me. See, I have gained two more talents.' His master said to him, 'Well done, good and faithful slave. You were faithful with a few things,

I will put you in charge of many things; enter into the joy of your master.'

"And the one also who had received the one talent came up and said, 'Master, I knew you to be a hard man, reaping where you did not sow and gathering where you scattered no *seed*. And I was afraid, and went away and hid your talent in the ground. See, you have what is yours.'

"But his master answered and said to him, 'You wicked, lazy slave, you knew that I reap where I did not sow and gather where I scattered no *seed*. Then you ought to have put my money in the bank, and on my arrival I would have received my *money* back with interest. Therefore take away the talent from him, and give it to the one who has the ten talents.'

"For to everyone who has, *more* shall be given, and he will have an abundance; but from the one who does not have, even what he does have shall be taken away. Throw out the worthless slave into the outer darkness; in that place there will be weeping and gnashing of teeth" (Matthew 25:14-30, emphasis added).

All three servants received abilities, but one failed to activate his. The two who used their talents created more, but the one who failed to initiate his lost even what he had. Through this parable, we discover that the Lord expects us to produce fruit with the power and abilities He has given us. Don't bury your talent – activate!

Aesthetics Attract Success

Natural considerations that create beauty and harmony in your world are also important in developing *realms* and *atmospheres* that create your world. For example, if you walked into a restaurant that had chipped and worn out furniture, old lighting with bulbs burned out, an odor of garbage, and dirty dishes piled high on the counters, you would probably decide to go elsewhere. They might have the best filet mignon in town, but few people will ever try it. Why? Their aesthetics create a realm of failure.

If you drive through the high-end area of your city, you will find the yards are well groomed, the streets are clean, the homes are in good repair and tastefully decorated. On the other hand, when driving through the poorest areas you often find homes in poor repair, broken vehicles and trash in yards and driveways. The aesthetics in the area contribute to the establishment of a realm.

I knew a single mom who lived in a poor area of town due to restricted budget. The house she could afford to rent was in poor repair, and her landlord refused to offer compensation to improve it. But she was determined to make this house her home and create a nice *atmosphere* in which to raise her children. She wrote down her "wish list" and prayed over it every day. She cleaned up the yard and repaired what she could. Before long, paint was given to them and with help from friends they painted the house inside and out. They didn't have much furniture but they fixed the home up to look adorable. Everything was neat and tidy inside and out. They swept sidewalks and porch, mowed the lawn, and planted a flower garden. Here was a little realm of paradise in their unkempt neighborhood.

You really noticed their house when you drove down the road. It was *different* from the others even though many other homes were the same age and model. They gave others on their street a vision of what could be done and before long others had fixed up their homes. This single mom led a few of her neighbors to the Lord. She had carved out a realm of hope in the neighborhood because of a coat of paint and a cleaned up yard. Aesthetics contribute to building *realms*! Most often the difference between a house and a home is simply aesthetics!

Some prisons are painting the walls of the cells pink, because they have discovered that the color pink creates an *atmosphere* of calmness. Colors create all kinds of effects, and that is why marketing psychologists study the influence of colors.

Bringing order into a messy office or home makes a difference to the *atmosphere*. When you have a mess in your house with things out of place, you feel uncomfortable and disgruntled until you clean it up. Then, suddenly, it is as if a fresh breeze has blown through your office or home, but all that happened was you put things in order.

This principle applies to both large and small things, important ones and even not-so-important ones. Everything is better when attractively presented, including the way you keep your area at work, how you present work assignments, and even how you serve ordinary food. Men or women who want to attract a spouse, job applicants, and others should apply aesthetics to their personal appearance. Aesthetics makes a difference … hmmm, think I'll go and clean my office right now.

13

KEY #11—THE POWER TO CREATE THROUGH ASSOCIATION

13

Key #11—The Power to Create Through Association

THE PEOPLE YOU "HANG WITH" GREATLY INFLUENCE YOUR LIFE.
Parents understand this. If your child's friends are rebellious, dis-
respectful, and dishonoring, then you know that your child could
be headed in that direction. On the other hand, if your child keeps
company with respectful, well-mannered, and wise friends, you have
peace regarding their social and behavioral development.

As a young Christian, I was hungry to learn about the Holy
Spirit and attended classes at my church on the gifts of the Spirit. At
class, I met others who were not only hungry to grow in the Spirit
but more seasoned and familiar with spiritual things. The more I
associated with them the more I grew in the things of Spirit. When
in fellowship, we shared testimonies and insights with each other
regarding what we had learned and experienced. A *realm* of anointing in exercising gifts of the Spirit grew and expanded through this
group of people, until most of our congregation came to believe in
and enjoy the benefits of God's supernatural power and the flow of
the spiritual gifts.

The Power of Like-Mindedness

When my husband and I attended a mission training program, we sat under wise, experienced, and anointed missionaries and received Bible instruction in Kingdom values, faith, evangelism, and care for the poor. Our fellow students were also hungry for truth and spiritual growth. We were all of the same heart and mind and, even though the training program was only six months long, immersion in this intense, missions-oriented, community environment created accelerated growth. We lived, ate, slept, and breathed missions for six months, day and night. We associated only with those of like mind and heart. It was a powerful season of development.

When we engaged in missions and evangelism outreaches following classroom instruction, we had significant fruit. The association with seasoned instructors and a spiritually hungry student body produced a *realm* of grace that we walked in daily and inhabited during the outreaches. Years later, I am still practicing the wisdom I learned in those early days of instruction. That affiliation carved out a *realm* of anointing for missions and evangelism that I continue to enjoy today.

How to Avoid Mistakes

In the *realm* of business, motivation instructors teach their students to glean from those who are already successful in their fields of interest. You can learn much from those who have gone before you.

Due to the availability of media, you can glean from the experiences, both failures and successes, of many seasoned leaders through books, audio teachings, video, social media, webinars, and webcasts. You can avoid errors that are common to your realms by learning from the mistakes of others. Niels Bohr wisely said, "An expert is a person who has made all the mistakes that can be made in a very narrow field." Learning from the "experts" will shrink your learning curve in any *realm*.

Be Insightful About Your Influencers

We find an example of the positive power of association in the Bible; Jesus discipled His followers primarily through association. He called the twelve to follow Him, and through their association with Him they became disciples and learned to do the "same works He did." The book of Acts provides an amazing example of the power that association had on Peter and John:

> Now as they observed the confidence of Peter and John and understood that they were uneducated and untrained men, they were amazed, and began to **recognize them as having been with Jesus** (Acts 4:13, emphasis added).

It will work the same way for you. The more time *you* spend with Jesus today, the more *you* will be like Him tomorrow and do the works that He did, and "even greater works," according to John 14:12.

It is important to watch over your associations, because wrong associations can potentially create destructive *realms* in your life. There will be some in your life who you are called to influence. There are individuals in my life that the Lord has called me to bless with His life and light, even though they presently walk and live in *realms* of bondage. However, I am careful not to "partner with" their negative *realms* but to only love and care about them. If I were to associate with their bondage, I

> The more time *you* spend with Jesus today, the more *you* will be like Him tomorrow and do the works that He did.

could find myself entangled in their *realm* of bondage rather than the freedom for which I was created.

You have probably heard the old proverb, "One bad apple spoils the bunch." This is speaking of the power of negative association. It is actually true that if you put one rotten apple in a bag with good ones, before long those around the rotten apple will also become rotten. The closer the apples are to the rotten one, the more vulnerable they are. Do you associate with appealing, yet "rotten," apples? Perhaps it is time to find a new tree to "hang out" in.

As Christians, it is important that we love the lost, the broken, and the bound; however, we must always remember who and whose we are. We are called to be *in the world* as a witness for Christ and yet not *of the world* (John 17:13-16). This means that we are to watch over the realms in which we live and walk. Because I am called to bring light to the darkness, I go into the darkness … but not to be a part of it. To bring light into darkness, I must live in the realm of light.

If darkness influences you, beware! Move away from its influence. You are in danger of creating a realm of darkness around your life that will become your world. Are there associations in your life that are having a negative influence on you? Are you partnering with negative *realms*? Are you being drawn in?

A movie production company hired a young executive who grew up in a Christian home. Before entering this company, she was a person of high morals, good friends, and she held to virtuous life values. However, within a year of working with co-workers who were partygoers and drug users, she began engaging in that lifestyle. It did not happen overnight, but little by little she let down her moral guard and entered "their world." She began living an immoral life, became addicted to crack cocaine, and within three years her life fell apart.

She left the production company a broken young woman. However, over time she was able to get her life back on track. She built new healthy relationships and watched carefully over her associations.

Keep good company! Your associations contribute to creating your world.

14

KEY #12—THE POWER TO CREATE THROUGH OVERCOMING

14

Key #12—The Power to Create Through Overcoming

You were created to create,
but you have enemies who will attempt to thwart you
and render you fruitless.
Let's identify some of those enemies.

Enemy #1 – Doubt and Unbelief

ALL THINGS ARE POSSIBLE IN GOD, and His promises to you are sure when you embrace them with *faith*. Without faith, there is no ability to unlock or implement the creative downloads required to change your world. Israel failed to enter the Promised Land due to the hardness of their hearts caused by doubt and unbelief. However, this evil duo will not have power to destroy your future, if you…

…believe God and believe in what He can do
in and through you!

The enemies of doubt and unbelief will always attack you when you move forward to create something awesome for the glory of God. In the year 2001, the Lord called our team to host an event that required the largest step of faith we had ever taken.

When we first received the vision, we calculated the costs and the budget was around $40,000. That was a stretch for us at the time, but we received confirmation this was from the Lord, so we resolved to do the project. After committing, the Lord further instructed us not to charge a registration fee for this event, and that meant we would have no finances to launch it. As we moved forward, we received further nudges from the Lord to enhance the event, and the budget swelled – doubling, tripling, and eventually reaching $250,000, including a $100,000 missions offering.

To be completely transparent with you – I freaked out a few times prior to the event. Because we were not taking registrations, we had no clue how many people were coming, and we didn't have the funds usually created by registration fees. God invited me to create a glorious event for Him, and yet waves of doubt and unbelief attacked me. With each wave, I went back to the Lord until His "blessed assurance" filled my heart once again.

When the event finally occurred, it was AMAZING! The fruit it produced was so abundant that even ten years afterward, I heard reports of how it transformed lives. However, it was a journey of faith from its inception to the very last session. When we tallied all the costs and income of the event, we had met every single penny of the budget. Glory to God!

We overcame the assaults of doubt and unbelief through faith, and as a result, the Lord invited us to host other events of that caliber. Each conference we hosted afterward was easier because we had created a history of faith in God. He was faithful to meet every need, every time. We experienced a promotion in our faith level!

These enemies, doubt and unbelief, hinder so many from creating glorious testimonies, experiences, and encounters. You can be a victor over doubt and unbelief.

This is the victory that has overcome the world – our faith
(1 John 5:4 NKJV).

Enemy #2 – Dragons of Discouragement

Endurance defeats discouragement. Endurance is often required before breakthrough comes. Many inventors had numerous failures before achieving success.

Walt Disney, a famous creator in the entertainment field, failed several times and even had a bankruptcy prior to originating the famous cartoon character, Mickey Mouse. He overcame discouragement and endured. He refused to give up, and his endurance paid off, didn't it? He continued to pursue his dreams, they came to pass, and Disneyland, Disney World, and Disney Productions have created *realms* and *atmospheres* of family entertainment. As Christians, we have the ability in Christ to fill the earth with godly influences. We must not allow the enemy of discouragement to tempt us to give up.

> The One who overcame every discouragement lives within you and He will give you strength and encouragement to achieve your purpose!

Our greatest example is Jesus, Himself. When He was creating a path to salvation for all mankind, it was not easy for Him. However, He would not allow the discouragement of slander, betrayal, denial, spiritual warfare, or even physical mistreatment to cause Him to give up. He endured to the end and secured the prize; *you* can do it too, because … the One who overcame every discouragement lives within you and He will give you strength and encouragement to achieve your purpose!

Enemy #3 – The Pitfall of Pride

Human pride sets you up for failure – "Pride goes before *destruction*, and a haughty spirit before a *fall*" (Proverbs 16:18 NKJV, emphasis added). We must always remember that *God gave us* the ability to create and be successful in our *realms*. It is His goodness and mercy that grants us the pleasure of creating with Him. It is never about us; it is *always* about Him. I have seen many people begin strong in the Lord but when they achieved a little success they became prideful and selfish. When pride is not broken, a fall is inevitable. Pride *always* destroys, so we must *always* embrace humility before God and before man, as Christ did!

Remember, as a co-creator with God, your greatest aim is love! To create your world, you must first overcome love's enemies.

Enemy #4 – Enemies of Love

Unforgiveness, bitterness, and jealousy have destroyed many dreams and dreamers. Love must be our greatest aim in life, because love is the *atmosphere* of heaven and a fundamental nature of God. In 1 Corinthians 13, Scripture teaches that without love we have nothing … are nothing … and even what we may accomplish profits for nothing.

Your greatest aim is love! To create your world, you must first overcome love's enemies.

Enemies of unforgiveness, bitterness, and jealousy oppose love and block the creative process by producing destructive *atmospheres*. I have known many gifted and talented individuals with tremendous potential who produced "things" that lacked godly value because they allowed the enemies of love to grip their souls. Unfortunately, the "things" they brought forth often created a mess that negatively affected many!

Enemy #5 – Contrary Mindsets

We often think of our enemy as the devil and, of course, he is. He stands for everything contrary to God's love and truth. We do not partner with him in any way. We only partner with God, and like Jesus, we have "loved righteousness and hated wickedness," and therefore are anointed "with the oil of joy above our fellows" (Hebrews 1:9).

However, your enemy is not only Satan but also every *thought* that opposes God's truth. Consequently, your greatest battle will be in your own mind – the place where contrary thoughts and mindsets make a stand against the truth of God. However, Scripture teaches that we have power over these mental strongholds, "For the weapons of our warfare are not carnal but mighty in God for pulling down strongholds" (2 Corinthians 10:4 NKJV).

Enemy #6 – Sin (Disobedience to God)

Sin is lethal! The Bible teaches that sin destroys, and there are many examples in Scripture of that truth. Individuals who embrace sin are disqualified from receiving the power and authority to change their worlds.

Earlier in the book, you learned that "the things you focus on, you empower." Consequently, focusing on not sinning never works. The solution is focusing on *doing* something right rather than *not doing* something wrong. When you focus on righteousness, sin will be far from you. Remain in the glorious presence of God's love and you will be far from sin, for *you cannot focus on two opposing thoughts at the same time.* Filling your mind with the righteousness of God WILL overcome sin.

Jesus overcame the temptations of the enemy in the wilderness. The devil used every weapon in his arsenal to snare Him, and Jesus was genuinely tempted, but He would not have it. Following that time of testing, Jesus began His ministry with great demonstrations of power (Matthew 4).

You, too, will be tempted, perhaps in many ways, but remember who you are – you are the righteousness of God in Christ Jesus and you have been set free from the law of sin and death (Romans 8:2). That means you truly have a choice. Sin no longer has authority or control; you *can* choose righteousness over sinfulness.

The person who is a successful creator of realms and atmospheres is an overcomer of sin, Satan, one's own mind and emotions – YOU are that person!

In Christ, you are called to be a victor – an overcomer. When you begin to step out in faith to create *realms* and *atmospheres* of God's blessings in your life, expect to be attacked by contrary situations, pressures, and temptations that seek to destroy your efforts. Jesus warned that, "The thief comes only to steal and kill and destroy; [however] I came that [you] may have life, and have it abundantly" (John 10:10). Remember that you *are* an overcomer in Christ! When you stand your ground as a victor, you will create strength and victory, and experience glorious promotion in the Spirit.

The person who is a successful creator of *realms* and *atmospheres* is an overcomer of sin, Satan, one's own mind and emotions – YOU are that person!

15

LET'S GET STARTED CREATING YOUR WORLD!

15

Let's Get Started Creating Your World!

You were reborn in Christ to be a creator of *realms* and *atmospheres*! In this book, I have shared many of the tools required to fulfill your purpose and enjoy a life beyond your wildest expectations. However, simply reading a book will not make you a creator. It is now time to begin activating your universe.

As I shared in a previous chapter, one of the greatest, most profound secrets to creating godly influence around you is simply abiding in Him.

Jesus said:

Abide in Me, and I in you. As the branch cannot bear fruit of itself unless it abides in the vine, so neither can you unless you *abide in Me*. I am the vine, you are the branches, *he who abides in Me* and I in him, he bears much fruit, for apart from Me you can do nothing (John 15:4-5, emphasis added).

Mary of Bethany knew this secret. She chose to take time away from her daily life and selected a better way – sitting at the feet of Jesus. That posture of adoration created an *atmosphere* of love and devotion to Christ. She carved out a realm of devotion and worship that multitudes have enjoyed throughout time and eternity.

You, also, have the power to create *realms* and *atmospheres* for His glory for all eternity. It all begins with your heart connecting to His. Everything we create that has eternal worth comes through abiding in Christ.

Guard Your Heart from "All Else"

You are the temple of the Holy Spirit and your entire being – spirit, soul, and body – is to be filled with the holy glory of the Lord. Realms of love, wisdom, knowledge, purity, and truth are to fill you to the exclusion of *all else*. "Guard your heart above *all else*, for it determines the course of your life" (Proverbs 4:23 NLT, emphasis added).

The world you create *around you* comes from what is *within you*. The fruit of your life springs forth from that which is in your heart.

The world you create *around you* comes from what is *within you*.

So, dear reader, draw close to Christ and let your relationship with Him be your greatest focus. His divine essence will flow from His glory and presence within you to create your world.

I'm excited for you and for the Kingdom. As you create an awesome world around you – a world of blessing, goodness, love, glory, abundance, and truth – you will be an instrument of God to cause His "Kingdom come and His will to be done on the earth as it is in heaven." Enjoy co-creating with your glorious God and King!

May your journey begin!

16

DO YOU KNOW YOUR CREATOR?

16

Do You Know Your Creator?

If you do not yet know Christ as your personal Savior and Lord, I would love to introduce you to Him. He is so beautiful, kind, and loving, and He desires to give you a brand new and eternal life in Him. He is knocking at the door of your heart right now and if you invite Him in, He will come.

If you desire to give your heart to Christ, and would like to invite Him to take full charge of your life, simply pray this prayer with heartfelt faith:

Dear Jesus, I confess my need of You. I believe that you died on the Cross for my sins and that you are alive forevermore as Savior and Lord. I repent from my wrongdoings and ask You to forgive me from all my sin and to cleanse me from all unrighteousness. By faith, I ask You to come into my heart and be my Savior and Lord. I give myself wholly to You! Amen!

Welcome to the family, the family of God!

He heard your prayer, and Christ did not hesitate to enter your heart. Regardless of what you felt or may not have felt, your name is now recorded in the Book of Life, and all the angels are rejoicing over your new birth in Christ.

To help you understand your salvation experience better, I am including a book called *God Loves You with An Everlasting Love*. If you read it through carefully, you will gain understanding of His love and how to walk with Him as a brand new creation.

BONUS BOOK:

God Loves You
With an Everlasting Love

1

The God Kind of Love

"Behold what *manner* of love the Father has bestowed on us, *that we should be called children of God*" (1 John 3:1 NKJV, emphasis added).

What manner of love would motivate a perfect, holy, and righteous God to offer a sinful, rebellious person the right to become His very own dear child and heir of all that He is and all that He has? It sounds like an extravagant act, doesn't it? This, however, is indeed the very manner of love the Father has shown to each and every one of us. Nothing throughout all the history of mankind has ever been able to make Him withdraw this love, although we have all put His love to the test over and over again. The demonstration of this love is unchangeable because He is unchangeable.

Many individuals regularly waver in their assurance of God's love and continually question their right standing with Him. The lack of this assurance breeds insecurity. They might ask, "Am I worthy enough? Do I love God enough? Am I performing well enough? Am I serving Him enough?"

My faith constantly wavered just like this before I understood the clear revelation of Christ's work on the Cross that demonstrated His eternal, unchangeable love for me. During those years, I always questioned my value in His sight. This produced striving, tension, and unrest. Without the assurance of His unchanging love, you are never free to be. If you are not free to be, you will never be free to do. It is the revelation of His love that produces fullness, freedom, and fruitfulness in life.

First John 4:16-19 teaches us that "There is no fear in love … We love, because He first loved us." When you understand the unconditional love of God, the fear of not being accepted and loved by Him is eliminated. You know deep within that you're His precious one, and you're assured of your place in His heart forever. When you have this type of assurance, even when everything in your life is unsettled, you feel secure. Love gives you an unshakeable confidence that He will work everything out and keep you in perfect peace.

Romans 8:32-39 informs us that the love the Father has given us is greater than any other force. It confidently assures us that nothing can separate us from His love. In fact, you can never be separated from the love of God that is in Christ Jesus – NEVER. In Christ, you are forever sealed in His holy love. Oh, how wonderful!

You probably weren't loved unconditionally in your childhood (just as others weren't), so from time to time lying thoughts might have assaulted your mind: I'm not loveable. I'm not accepted. I haven't been able to accomplish enough. I have no value. I can't succeed.

The Word, however, says that you are perfectly loved, and nothing at all can ever separate you from it. When you really start to understand this truth, you will be able to cast down the tormenting lies of rejection, inferiority, and insecurity. The power of God's love and favor will prevail, causing the lies to fall. Then you will experience what you were created to be from the foundation of the world – an object of His deep love and affection.

God wants you to feel so secure in His love that you will be able to go anywhere, do anything, face any spirit of rejection, and overcome any obstacle. You will be able to say with confidence, "I am a precious, loved child of God. I am His favored one."

Love is God's mark on our lives. Not only are we to know His love for ourselves, but we are to extravagantly share it with others. Once you know you are a loved one, His love in you will spill out all over the place and touch others – you won't be able to help it! This type of love doesn't come from an inward striving to be a loving person. It comes from knowing who you are as a perfectly loved child. Then His powerful grace flows through you like a river and offers refreshing to those around you.

A Personal Testimony

I remember so clearly what life was like without Christ and the revelation of His love. I was a young career woman, a wife, and mother of two boys, yet totally unfulfilled and broken. Most of my brokenness, however, was hidden to the onlooker. I wore an invisible mask of well-being, because I was afraid to let people see the real me. What if they rejected me? How could I ever cope with that? I constantly lived behind the many disguises that concealed the guilt and shame that plagued my heart regularly. I was in an invisible prison and I couldn't escape.

I tried everything to become free. I attended numerous self-help courses and joined new age/occult enlightenment groups, hoping to find some answers for my distressed soul. I regularly imbibed a variety of addictive substances in an effort to find comfort and relief. I also attempted to find meaning for life through work, career, and taking extra college courses. Every effort failed terribly to offer any liberty. I became increasingly unstable emotionally, with no way to get a grip on things. The more I tried, the more I failed. The more I failed, the more discouraged and bound I became. The tentacles of fear, shame, and guilt wrapped themselves around me, continuously strangling any tinge of hope. I was constantly plagued with a sense of powerlessness in life.

I was a mess and totally out of control! I desperately needed help but didn't know where to turn. God hears the cries of our heart, and He definitely heard mine. It was following a near-death experience, at the lowest point of my life, that the Lord sent a wonderful man to share the gospel with me. He was an Anglican minister named Reverend Ron Hunt. I will never forget the first evening I attended the little home Bible study at his invitation. Although I was nervous to step into that unfamiliar environment, I was pleasantly surprised as I witnessed a sincere group of people who obviously knew God in a very personal way. One after another that evening, they shared testimonies of how Jesus had changed their lives. They claimed that He forgave their sins, cleansed them from guilt and shame, and offered them a brand new life. Wow! That was exactly what I wanted ... but was it possible?

Following the meeting, I went home and while alone, kneeling on my living room floor, I cried out to this unseen God for help. "Jesus, I have nothing to offer You except my brokenness. I have made a big mess of my life, but I would really like You to come into my heart and make me new – just like You did for those people up the street." I honestly did not know if Jesus would want to come into my life or not. I felt so evil and had no confidence that He would be able to love the likes of me. Yet, to my amazement, He didn't hesitate to enter my heart. I hadn't even finished praying when I literally felt the presence of liquid love come into my being. The One who knew every wicked detail of my life didn't hesitate for a moment to show me His extravagant mercy and acceptance. I felt the pressure of my sin leave me, along with all the guilt and shame. It was as though a prison door had been opened, and I was allowed to run free. I felt lovely and beautiful inside for the very first time I could remember.

All I could do was cry. In fact, I cried all night while I worshipped Him. No one had to teach me to worship – when you are deeply touched by His love, worship is just a normal response ... it is the only response! Everything in you is so thankful, so grateful. I knew beyond a shadow of a doubt that this gift of love had nothing to do with my own ability to fix myself. I had already proven through constant failed attempts that I was "unfixable." This gift had nothing to do with me. This was a free gift of life – His gift of everlasting, unbendable, unchangeable, unshakable, and unfailing love! Yeah, God!

The next number of years were extremely fulfilling for me as I daily experienced increased revelation of His Word and His ways. His love healed, delivered, and established me in a brand new life. It had nothing at all to do with my efforts. This new life was His gift. It is a gift that can't be earned and it is available to everyone. It is available to you!

I began to serve the Lord with passion. I never for a moment felt a pressure to serve Him – I served Him because I loved Him. It's what you do when you're in love. My entire life changed. I had new friends, new interests, and new desires. I wanted to spend my entire life serving the One who had loved me so perfectly. Year after year was filled with a continual unfolding of His goodness.

In my experience as a young Christian, I had never tasted "legalism" (legalism is an attempt to secure right standing with the Lord through obedience to the Law). I was first introduced to this type of religious bondage when our family served the Lord on a foreign mission field (my husband began following Jesus a year after me). The leaders of the mission center were very passionate for the Lord, and I know they meant well. Unfortunately, they did not understand that the Lord's unconditional love is a gift and cannot be earned through our works. As a result, they taught those they worked with to perfect themselves through self-effort in order to please God. The leaders themselves also lived under this same burden. I experienced a daily performance pressure on this mission field.

In all my striving to do well, I constantly believed I was falling short of what was expected. I was convinced I was disappointing God, and the more I tried to please Him the more I failed. The more I failed, the more I strove within. The cycle continued with increasing despair. This type of pressure was bringing me right back into the torment and bondage I experienced prior to knowing Christ. I was plagued with the same guilt and the same shame. It simply showed up wearing different clothes. One was a cloak of unrighteousness, and the other was one of self-righteousness. Both were deadly and bore the same fruit of devastation.

After serving on this mission field as faithfully and diligently as I could for over six months, I finished our term feeling spiritually bankrupt. I had even lost assurance of my salvation. I believed I had totally failed the Lord and that He would never have any use for me again. I believed that I was no longer a precious child to Him – I had disappointed Him too deeply. What a deception I had stepped into!

On my return home from this mission experience, some friends helped me to rightly divide the Word and to trust that the Lord still loved me. The healing and restoration did not come overnight. At times, I was still plagued with the fear of being rejected by God and I constantly battled self-condemnation. I cried out constantly for relief. All I wanted was to feel close to God – to feel worthy of His love and to know I was pleasing Him.

It was years later that I finally received a revelation of the Cross. This revelation delivered me from the torment and fear that had bound my soul and became an anchor for my faith forever. The revelation of the Cross and the covenant Christ made with God on our behalf is an absolute foundation for understanding His unconditional love. The day I received this revelation, I wept for hours on end, completely in awe of His loving-kindness – completely amazed at His grace.

It is one thing to be touched by the love of God and enjoy the experience of it, like I had as a young Christian. It is another thing, however, to be fully anchored in the unshakable, unfailing revelation of the doctrine of His unconditional love. Jesus said, "You will know the truth, and the truth will make you free" (John 8:32). The day the revelation of the doctrine of the Cross filled my heart was the day I knew I would walk free forever. Regardless of what circumstances surrounded my life, regardless of how many condemning thoughts my mind received, I now had an eternal place to stand. I was anchored forever in His love because I understood the truth of it! I am blood-bought into an eternal love covenant that can never be broken. What freedom this truth brings!

In this writing, I am committed to introducing you to this life-changing, life-sustaining doctrine. May you come to know the revelation of this truth so deeply within your heart that your entire being will forever be filled and anchored in it. I desire you to walk through the following pages with expectation and focus as the Holy Spirit unfolds the most profound and life-altering doctrine in the entire Bible – the Cross and the Covenant. This doctrine reveals God's true heart of unfailing, tested love. He loves you with an everlasting love. He really does. You will see!

2

God Chose You!

God wanted you! You weren't a mistake, regardless of the circumstances that surrounded your birth. Perhaps you weren't planned by your parents, or maybe your conception was the result of an unfortunate incident. Even in cases as sad as these, you need to know that God had you in His heart from before the foundation of the world. He planned you. His ultimate desire was for you to be conceived and brought forth in a beautiful, pure atmosphere of parental love and affection. Tragically, everyone has fallen short of His perfect ways because of our sinful, imperfect nature. God planned for you to come forth into the realm of time and fulfill His eternal purpose for your life. His potential in you is fun to explore.

God actually wanted to have a family. That's why most folks desire to have children; that desire comes from Him. Mankind has been created in His likeness and, therefore, when you find yourself longing to have children, you are simply identifying with His passion. He wanted children, and that's why you do, too (unless you've been emotionally wounded or have a special call to remain single).

In the beginning, God created trees, flowers, birds, fish, animals, and a host of other earthly and celestial things. He loved everything He created and each day He said, "It is good." Even though He was very pleased, He still longed for a precious creation made in His likeness – an object of His affection to fulfill the longing of His righteous heart. My husband Ron and I did not have children in our first year of marriage. We did, however, have pets – two dogs.

Although we enjoyed our dogs and they were like family, they did not satisfy our longing for children. The dogs were nice, but not that nice. There was something inside us that said, "Children, children, children." That longing was a small taste of what the Lord felt in His heart for us. The dogs and other creatures were not enough for Him, either. Although He took pleasure in them, they did not satisfy His desire to have YOU! Passionate desire for you was burning inside His heart. Envisioning you, He said, "I long for you; I desire to pour out My deep love, kindness, and goodness upon you."

God deeply desired children, yet before man was ever created, God knew we were going to blow it. He wasn't caught off guard, though – He is the all-knowing One. As a result of knowing ahead of time about our sinful failures, before He even created us He initiated a plan to rescue our lives from the power of sin. This act is called "redemption" in the Bible. He actually took care of the problem for us before we had even acted out the problem (The Lamb was slain before the foundation of the world – Revelation 13:8). God has never been caught off guard by mankind's failures – and that includes yours!

Years ago, I said to the Lord, "I wouldn't choose to have children if I knew ahead of time they were going to rebel, betray, and dishonor me. I would be much happier without that type of child! Why then did You create us?" He spoke this clear word to me:

My plan was to prove to mankind that My love would withstand every resistance. I allowed My love to be tested so that you would know it would always stand and never be withdrawn. I am Love.

When anyone chooses to come into relationship with Me,
they will never ever need to doubt My love for them. Knowing
I passed every test, they will feel completely secure – and
that is My desire.

That's how much He loves you. Isn't that amazing? Behold, what manner of love is this?

The Cross and the Covenant

God's plan for you is to have an eternal relationship with Him that is established through a covenant. A covenant is a legally binding agreement between two people or parties. In order for a covenant to work, there needs to be absolute integrity in the making and the keeping of all its terms. Entering a covenant with a person of integrity gives you a sense of protection, a sense of security.

That's what the marriage covenant is supposed to be like. When you vow to be faithful to one another, to care for one another, and honor each other, you should feel a sense of belonging and oneness with your covenant partner. That is the purpose of covenant. It legally secures relationship.

Mankind does not have a history of being good covenant keepers, so the very thing that should offer security is making many feel insecure. Some don't even bother getting married anymore because they think it might last or it might not. That is one reason why there is so much breakdown in the family these days. There are broken covenants everywhere, and this is evidenced by the high divorce rate in our nation. God, however, is a covenant-keeping God. He is full of integrity and always keeps the terms of the covenants He makes.

The original use of the word covenant was, "where the blood flows." Ancient covenants always set terms, exchanged names, weapons, and resources. These covenants almost always included the consummation of the covenant through the mingling of blood. A covenant meal was served at the end of the ceremony and a celebration of this union commenced.

The marriage covenant is a blood covenant much like this. We make our vows before witnesses (which is an exchanging of terms), we exchange names (the bride usually takes her husband's name), and we exchange our resources (the assets of one, legally become the other's, in most cases). The marriage is then consummated through the sexual act, which breaks the hymen membrane (the shedding of blood). God's covenant plan for His relationship with man was a blood covenant (Christ's blood shed for us at the Cross). He set the terms, (through the Old Testament Law and Prophets) and then defined a name exchange (Jesus said, "In my name ask ..."), a weapons exchange (Jesus' weapons and armor are ours), and a resource exchange (all our needs are met through Him).

In ancient civilizations, a representative of one tribe would cut covenant with a representative of another tribe. When the two leaders cut covenant on behalf of their people, then their entire tribe enjoyed the benefits of the covenant. This is what Christ did for us when He represented mankind in a covenant with God. Jesus Christ was and is our covenant representative and leader. It is His responsibility, as our covenant representative, to keep all the terms for us. In exchange, we receive all the covenant blessings. Wow!

3

THE AMAZING GOOD NEWS

What I'm about to share with you is amazing. God desired to make a covenant with man that would secure us in relationship with Him for all eternity. However, He knew that once mankind fell, we would never keep a covenant. It was impossible because man became filled with a sin nature. To fulfill the covenant terms, God required a sinless representative for man who would keep all the conditions, but there was not a sinless person to be found. As a result, He chose to fill this position Himself. He chose to take our place in covenant by becoming a man. Jesus also took God's place in covenant because He is God. He is both man and God. In reality then, He was cutting covenant with Himself. This is how God could cut an eternal, unbreakable, unfailing covenant with man. Jesus, who was fully God, left heaven and came into the sinful world as a man in order to fulfill this plan.

Many Christians don't understand this, so I pray the light will go on for you today, because this truth is glorious. When you understand, you will worship and serve Him in full abandonment for all He has done. God loves you so much. He desires relationship with you even more than you desire relationship with Him. He knew you couldn't keep a covenant, so He determined to become man and fulfill both sides of the covenant Himself. Jesus, the Son of God and

Son of Man, made a covenant to include you in eternal relationship because you couldn't do it.

When He came as a man, He had to fulfill all of man's covenant terms which were laid out in Old Testament Law. If He failed to fulfill every point of the Law, or if He gave in to temptation just once, He would not qualify to keep the covenant on man's behalf. This would have been devastating for us, but there was an even greater risk for Him. Jesus is referred to in Scripture as the last Adam. The first Adam was a perfect man before the fall. He was made in God's image and likeness. When he fell into temptation, the rule and dominion that had been given to him was surrendered over to Satan. Romans 6:16 teaches that when we submit ourselves to sin, we become sin's slave. This is what happened to Adam when he submitted to Satan's temptation, and this is what would have happened to the last Adam (Jesus), too, if He fell into even the slightest temptation. Only pure love would be willing to take a risk like that.

Jesus the Man

Jesus came just like the first Adam. He was of man's nature yet without sin. He was to fulfill man's requirement in covenant – with man's power and with man's capabilities. The Holy Spirit came upon Him to empower Him, just like the Holy Spirit empowers you today. Through the power of the Holy Spirit, the man, Jesus, remained sinless throughout His entire life on the earth. You need to understand that He resisted sin in man's strength, with the power of the Holy Spirit helping Him. You'd better believe that there was a huge wrestle in His soul against sin, even though He was perfect and without sin in His nature. He had to wrestle just like the first Adam, because He had to secure the victory as a man in order to restore mankind to his rightful place in relationship with God. Ultimately, Jesus Christ, at the end of His "covenant course," would be acknowledged not only as a perfect God but also as a perfect Man who would sit on a throne at the right hand of God. All things in heaven and in earth would ultimately be summed up in Him.

It was not easy for Christ to resist sin. In fact, at one point it was so grueling that He sweat drops of blood in His resistance against the temptations (Hebrews 12:4). He did it in man's power for you so you wouldn't have to do it, because you couldn't do it. Everything required for mankind to enter covenant with God was fulfilled through the man Jesus Christ. Jesus fulfilled all the Law and the Prophets.

Jesus Counts the Cost

Before the foundation of the world, Jesus probably had to ask Himself, "How big is My love? Am I willing to perform acts of love, kindness, and mercy for people who don't even desire Me? Am I able to love so deeply that I would actually become sin for those whom I love? Am I willing to taste death for them?" He counted the cost and made a love choice with you in mind, saying, "Oh, yes! You are worth everything to Me. I will gladly leave heaven and pay the price, with joy!"

Jesus Arrives on Earth

Mary, a young virgin, conceived Jesus by the power of the Holy Spirit. She and Joseph traveled to Bethlehem, where Mary went into labor. There was no available lodging, so Mary gave birth in an animal stable and laid baby Jesus in a feeding trough. What kind of treatment was this for man's Savior? No palace, no special treatment, and hardly anyone even discerned who He was.

He had to start passing love tests right away. If He had been offendable, He could have thought: *Well, that's it, I'm going back to heaven. I tried to do something nice for you, but you treated Me like an animal and threw Me in a feeding trough.* Jesus, however, did not take offense. In tremendous humility, He passed the love test. Even though He was worthy of the most extravagant treatment, He didn't demand it or expect it. He came to serve.

Herod even tried to have Him killed as a baby, but Jesus never stopped loving. He never withdrew love and never lost faith. What would you do if your only motivation was to help people and all of a sudden they're trying to kill you? You'd probably say something like, "I don't need you. I'll go somewhere else." But Jesus had a different heart.

His Ministry Begins

His childhood passed and His ministry began. He taught in the synagogues as a rabbi. The religious leaders examined His teachings carefully. They knew the Scriptures and were considered experts in the Word of God and doctrine. Jesus, however, is true doctrine. He is the living Word. He is true theology and yet He was called a blasphemer and a heretic by these very leaders. They attempted to bring legal charges against Him. This is the way they treated the true God.

How would you feel if you were God? There you are, teaching truth right from heaven. You're speaking truth because you *are* truth, and the people you came to save are saying, "You're a liar. You're a deceiver. You're a heretic. You're teaching us false doctrine. You're demonized." Character assaults like this are much worse than simply saying, "Your theology is off."

I've experienced a little of that resistance myself and I must say those times were brutal. Everything in me wanted to withdraw. Jesus, however, never withdrew love from us, not for a moment. Each time He was opposed or mistreated by man, His love once again passed the test. He said, "I will never withdraw love and I will never stop believing in what can happen in your life." He kept consistent in faith and love through all the mistreatment.

Jesus chose twelve disciples and then seventy-two. He poured His time and life into them by giving, teaching, and mentoring day in and day out. Many others also followed His ministry. His own didn't always treat Him well, but even with all the disappointments He suffered, He never wavered in His commitment to them.

4

LOVE'S GREATEST TESTS

The Garden of Gethsemane

One of Christ's most excruciating struggles was in Gethsemane (Gethsemane means "the oil press"). He faced every temptation that man would ever encounter. Strong forces of hell were spiritually assaulting Him. As we established earlier, Jesus had to resist sin as a man – in the same strength as the first Adam. You were in His heart the entire time He was wrestling against temptation. The pressure was so great against His soul that He sweat blood in His resistance against sin. With every drop of blood that pushed through His bursting capillaries He was saying, "For you, I will resist. No matter what it feels like. No matter how excruciating it is. My emotions are being rung out beyond explanation, but it's all for you. It's all for you."

I've faced some grueling spiritual battles and have engaged in warfare with powerful demonic entities. Although these seasons were unbearably painful, they were nothing at all in comparison to what Jesus experienced. I am a little aware, however, of the crushing feeling that pressures your emotions and your mind during such times. In the midst of this type of battle, it is essential to keep focused, because all you have is the Word of God to stand on. When everything else that is going on in your life seems contrary to the truth, there's just one point of choice: "I will stand on Your Word, Lord, no matter what. I will trust my soul into Your keeping." It is all you have. At the end of these battles, your emotions, your thinking processes, and even your physical body is weakened, fatigued, and fragile. At times during these intense battles, I had to draw strength from God to even breathe. The impact of such warfare is very excruciating; I can't even find words to describe it. What I experienced, however, is still nothing in comparison to the pressure that Jesus experienced.

What was it like for Jesus when He had the hordes of hell trying to take Him out? What motivated Him to stand through this agony? God didn't *need* to put Himself in this position. Do you know why He did? It was His love for you. He said, "I'm doing this to fulfill your covenant requirements." He loves you that much. Just for a moment, forget about everyone else on the face of the earth. If you alone were left, He'd do it all over again. In the midst of Gethsemane's agony, you were in His vision. The thought of having you with Him for all eternity was His motivation to continue. Your face gave Him the strength to endure.

Betrayed by a Friend

When Jesus departed from the garden, He was weak and exhausted. Judas, one of His twelve disciples, approached Him, betraying Him with a kiss. Even though Jesus knew Judas would betray Him, He continued to call him friend. He said, "Friend, do what you have come for" (Matthew 26:50). Betrayal is very painful. If you have been betrayed, you know how difficult this is on your emotions, but even betrayal could not make Jesus withdraw love or friendship. There is nothing you can do to make Him withdraw His love. You can treat God terribly. You can tell Him to leave you alone, but He will never withdraw love from you. He'll continue to say, "I love you."

Abandoned and Denied

I can't imagine what it would feel like to be in a ferocious spiritual battle and then experience betrayal by a close friend and co-worker. To top it all off though, all His followers fled when He was arrested. When you're in a hard place, being falsely accused, you just want someone, even if it's only one, to stand with you. *Is there one that will just come to My side right now? Is there one who will believe in Me? Is there one who will defend Me?* Jesus did not even have one. His own disciples, whom He had poured into for three years, all fled in fear of their reputation.

As Jesus was led away, He heard Peter, one of His closest disciples, swearing, "No, I never knew Him." Oh how painful it must have been for Jesus when He heard that denial. He knew prophetically that Peter would do this, but foreknowledge doesn't ease the emotional devastation when it actually happens.

> *Peter, I need you right now. Are you so afraid for your own life that you wouldn't even admit you know Me? Peter, look into My eyes and see My pain. See My love. You have denied Me, but You cannot make Me withdraw love from you.*

His Trial

False witnesses were paid to testify against Jesus in court. That is harsh! When you know someone is lying about you, the natural tendency is to immediately defend yourself. Isaiah 53:7 reveals, though, that Jesus was like a lamb led to the slaughter, silent before His shearers, not opening His mouth in His own defense. He had purposed in His heart to offer unconditional love and mercy toward the lying witnesses.

You can line your pockets with filthy lucre, but you cannot make Me withdraw My love from you.

They stripped Him naked, placed a crown of thorns on His head and mocked Him openly. Even though you and I were not yet created, we were there, hidden in the heart of depraved humanity. We might think that we would never hurt or deny Him but, like Peter, we might not understand the weakness of our own flesh. It is probable that each of us would have done the same thing.

Christ's love was being severely tested by mankind. You and I have put His love to the test many times, and yet He has never abandoned us and neither has He withdrawn love. He never will.

Beaten and Scourged

Jesus was beaten, spit upon and, mocked. His face was violently struck, apparently making Him unrecognizable. Again, with every cruel punch, His response was only love as He gazed into the eyes of His afflicters.

He was brutally scourged with a whip that had nine leather strips. At the end of each strip were little pieces of sharp metal or bone. Each stroke provided nine lashings. It was a common belief that 40 lashes would bring death. Under Roman laws He might have received even more. History reveals that His flesh was literally ripped open and that His innards were exposed. Every time the razor-sharp edge of the whip dug into His flesh, you were in His heart. Your face was constantly before Him. You were the reason He could endure such hostility. Looking into the face of those who were cruelly scourging Him, He would have said once again, "You cannot make Me withdraw My love." He would have assured you, too, if it was your hand holding the scourge.

Crucified

Jesus carried the heavy wooden cross that was heaved onto His back. Weakened with pain, He staggered up to Calvary's hill. An angry mob followed Him, mocking, ridiculing and shouting, "Crucify Him, crucify Him." They nailed His hands and feet to the cross and hung Him between two guilty criminals. They were crucifying an innocent man.

To many, it looked like Jesus' life was being taken. It appeared that Jesus was defeated, but His life wasn't taken – *it was given!* The devil did not take Jesus' life. The false witnesses did not take His life. The Jews did not kill Him. The Romans did not kill Him. You did not kill Him. No one killed Him. He freely gave His life. When you see Jesus hanging on the cross, you see Love Himself hanging there – a free gift of love – love that had been completely proven and tested against everything that could possibly oppose or destroy it.

Love Himself was on that cross, stripped naked and humiliated, hanging there in agonizing pain. In the midst of this agony, one of the thieves asked to be saved. Jesus didn't hesitate. In His greatest point of need, He continued to pour Himself out. He could have said, "What do you mean, you want a favor from Me? Really? I don't deserve to be here, and you do. Forget it, it's too late!" Jesus wasn't and isn't like that. He proved His love once again: "Of course, I will save you. In fact, today I'll do it and you will be with Me in paradise. You will see the glory of My salvation."

Looking down from His cross, Jesus saw a mass of people – a crowd who delighted to watch Him die. "If You're the Son of God, come down off that cross and save Yourself." His merciful, loving retaliation was, "Father, forgive them; for they do not know what they are doing" (Luke 23:34).

Can you imagine? We sometimes find it difficult to forgive those who hurt or offend us. Consider Jesus: a mass of angry people rallied against Him, and you were there, too – all humanity was. Oh yes, He saw your face in the crowd that day. We all sinned against Him, and yet He said, "Father, forgive them all." He forgave all the sins of mankind right at that point. He cancelled the debt of sin. Only pure Love Himself can do that.

He went even further and actually became mankind's sin. Jesus chose to become sin. He chose to have your sin poured into Him so that He could pour His righteousness into you. He chose to become something abhorrent that would be judged, so you would be free from judgment. Have you ever been mistreated, taken advantage of, or sinned against? Doesn't it give you a great feeling to see the offender punished, knowing they're getting what they deserve? But Jesus' heart was different. He said, "No, I'll take the punishment for your sin. I'll take full responsibility. You can go free."

A number of years ago, I was on the mission field. I misjudged a particular situation and consequently made some bad decisions. My actions seriously hurt some individuals. When I finally saw the situation clearly, I was terribly grieved, overwhelmed, and deeply ashamed. I thought: I should have known better, I shouldn't have done that. It was difficult for me to believe that I hadn't seen the situation through eyes of wisdom in the first place. I asked for forgiveness from one individual who was particularly wounded through the process. They refused to extend the undeserved mercy that I desperately needed. For years afterward, I had a very difficult time forgiving myself.

One day, I was crying out to the Lord in prayer, "Don't let my failure continue to hurt them. Don't let it ruin their lives." I felt terrible to the very core of my being.

The Lord spoke very soberly to me, "You didn't commit that sin. You didn't make that mistake. I did."

"What? No, Lord! You never did that. I'm the one who did it."

"I did it," He insisted.

"Jesus, no You didn't. You are perfect and You have never wronged anyone, ever!"

He tenderly responded, "I bore your mistake on the Cross 2,000 years ago. I chose to take full responsibility for this mistake so that you might go free. I have even borne the judgment for it. You are free! I became this sin for you and, in exchange I have given you My righteousness. This has all been paid in full. If there is any further problem, that hurting individual will need to come to Me. You have been totally released and fully justified. You never did it!"

I burst into tears, tears of gratitude that flowed from deep inside my being. How can I not love a God who showed that much mercy? He clearly revealed to me that day that this is what He's done for us all. This is what is called "substitution." He literally took our judgment and in exchange, gave us His life and righteousness. Oh my, can we fully grasp this?

5

FOR ALL PEOPLE AND FOR ALL TIME

God's love for us today is no different than it was for the sinful crowd at the foot of the cross 2,000 years ago. He performed an eternal exchange, saying, "It is no longer you that sinned, but Me. I have become your sin. I have paid the penalty. I have taken full responsibility. It is no longer your issue." Love laid down His life for all people. Love laid down His life for you! You are free!

Dying in Faith

Gazing at you through the portals of time, Jesus died on the cross in love and in faith. He gave up the ghost and cried out, "It is finished." Helpless, but remaining in faith, He entrusted His life into the hands of His Father. When He became your sin, He had no power to raise Himself from the dead. God planned Christ's resurrection before the foundation of the world. And Jesus believed Him.

After His death, Jesus descended into the lower parts of the earth. On the third day, His heavenly Father raised Him from the dead. Mary and the other women, the disciples and many others literally saw Him walking the earth following His resurrection. Oh yes, He is the Resurrection and the Life – the First Born from the dead! When He was raised from the dead, He took the keys of death and of hell. He stripped the devil of his authority and made an open show of him. Oh, what an eternal victory!

Jesus Christ Is Forever the Resurrection and the Life.

Jesus has invited everyone into eternal relationship with God through simply receiving Him as Savior by faith. All the work for mankind's redemption has been completed in Christ – finished! He did it all for us. The only thing left for us to do is to simply believe. Mankind's identity is found in Jesus – the One who accomplished everything for us. No man can boast in his own ability to save himself. Jesus fully paid the debt that we could not pay. He fully accomplished the work that we could not do. All glory to Him!

Jesus walked the earth for 40 days after His resurrection from the dead and then gloriously ascended to heaven. He is forever seated at the right hand of God, far above all principalities, powers, and every name that is named (Ephesians 1:20-22). We are seated with Jesus in the heavenly places when we receive Him as our Savior (Ephesians 2:6). Our life is hidden with God in Christ (Colossians 3:3).

Sealed in the Covenant

Everyone who believes in Christ has the gift of everlasting life – His abundant life. Everyone who believes in Him is forever sealed into covenant, a legally binding love agreement between God and man. This covenant is an eternal covenant. It is impossible for it to be broken because it is between Jesus, Man and Jesus, God. Jesus won our place for us through His own sinless life. When you believe in Him, you are saved from the separation from God that sin creates. Your identity as a Kingdom child is not in your own ability to accomplish anything. It is in His completed work – His ability – past tense. It is done! It is finished!

In fact, if we were to be absolutely honest right now, you are an utter failure outside of Christ. It is impossible for you to please God in your own strength – absolutely impossible! The only way anyone can please God is by believing in Christ. The arms of Jesus are open to all sinners. If you receive Jesus as Savior, then your identity is in Him. You are in Christ, a brand new creation. You are eternally one with Him. It is simple faith that connects you to this glorious eternal salvation. That's all you have to do – simply believe. That's it. That's all. Ephesians 2:8-9, says "For by grace you have been saved through faith; and that not of yourselves, it is the gift of God; not as a result of works, that no one may boast."

What is this grace that saves us? It is His divine influence in your life. It is His choice to accomplish everything for you. It is His work of favor over you – undeserved favor. You don't deserve it, I don't deserve it. No one does. It's undeserved, unmerited favor. It's His influence that comes upon your heart. You have been saved by grace through faith. Simple faith is what connects you to the glorious, finished work of the Cross. When you make this "faith connection," you become a brand new creation. 2 Corinthians 5:17 states, "Therefore, if anyone *is* in Christ, *he is* a new creation; old things have passed away; behold, all things have become new" (NKJV).

Ah, what a glorious life we have been given in Christ – a brand new life, an eternal relationship with God Himself. Christ did all this for YOU! You see how precious you are? God loves you with an everlasting love ... He really does!

Perhaps you have just read this through, and your heart is longing to become God's child. It's simple. The following is a little prayer. If it represents your desire, why don't you go ahead and pray it from your heart. God will hear you. His gift of life and love will enter you, and your journey begins!

Dear Heavenly Father,

Thank You for loving me so perfectly through Your Son, Jesus Christ, and for offering me eternal life through the finished work of the Cross. I turn away from a self-ruled life and invite Jesus Christ to enter my heart as my personal Savior and Lord.

Come into my life, Lord Jesus, and forgive me of all my sin. Give me new life within and make me the person You want me to be. I believe that You are now in my heart and my new life has begun. I now belong to You. You are my God. Thank You, Father. AMEN.

Your New Life Begins

When you receive Jesus as your personal Savior by faith, His life enters your spirit. You are now what the Scripture calls *born again* (Read John 3:1-9). You have Christ's brand new life inside you. His purity, love, peace, truth, and blessings are now inside your spirit. You are so beautiful and perfect within.

Just like a new baby in the natural needs nourishment and care, so do new babies in the Lord. The Bible is full of truth that is like fresh milk and food for you. As you read it each day, it will nourish you and reveal wonderful things about God's love and His ways. You will also want to meet some other Christians who understand the love of God. Fellowshipping with other followers of Jesus is so much fun. Take some time and visit some churches in your area. Christ's Holy Spirit dwells within you, and He will direct you to a good fellowship if you ask Him to.

As a child of your heavenly Father, you are invited to communicate with Him through prayer. Prayer is easy – you simply share your heart with Him. He loves to answer your desires. Some good teachings on prayer will help you to grow in the many different ways that you can communicate with God. Prayer is very fulfilling and powerful.

All of God's goodness belongs to you when you are in Christ ... so imbibe of it all. You have been called to a full and glorious life in Jesus. Enjoy!

6

A Decree

Proclaim this decree often over your life!

The Lord loves me with an everlasting love and has promised to give me a future and a hope. With lovingkindness, He has drawn me unto Himself. I look carefully and intently at the manner of love the Father has poured out upon me. It is through this love that He has called me to be His dear child. I am completely and fully accepted in Him, my God and Savior. Nothing can separate me from the love of God that is in Christ Jesus my Lord – not tribulation or distress, not persecution, famine or nakedness, not peril, sword, angels, principalities, powers, death, or life; neither things present nor things to come – absolutely nothing can separate me from the love of God which is in Christ Jesus my Lord.

God's love toward me is patient and kind. His love for me bears all things, believes all things, hopes all things and endures all things. His love will never fail. His love for me is so rich that He gave His only begotten Son. Because of this, I will never perish but have everlasting life with Him. As a result of God's great love for me, I have an unbreakable, eternal covenant with Him. Through this covenant of love, He has put His laws within my heart and written His commandments upon my mind.

ᴉ have been invited to the Lord's banqueting table, and His ban-
er over me is love! His love is better than the choicest of wines.
Through His intimate love, He draws me and invites me to follow after Him. I am fair and pleasant unto Him. I am rooted and
grounded in His love, well able to comprehend with all believers the
width and length and depth and height of His unfailing love. I have
been called to know this rich love that surpasses knowledge so that I
may be filled with all the fullness of God.

I truly am the object of God's deepest love
and affection.

Patricia King

Patricia King is president of XP Ministries and co-founder of XPmedia.com, Inc. She has been a pioneering voice in ministry, with over 30 years of background as a Christian minister in conference speaking, prophetic service, church leadership, and television & radio appearances. Patricia has written numerous books, produced many CDs and DVDs, hosts the TV program "Patricia King–Everlasting Love," and is the CEO of a number of businesses. Patricia's reputation in the Christian community is world-renowned.

Christian Services Association (CSA) was founded in Canada in 1973 and in the USA in 1984. It is the parent ministry of XP Ministries, a 501-C3 founded in Arizona. They are located in Maricopa, AZ and Kelowna, B.C. Patricia King and numerous team members equip the body of Christ in the gifts of the Spirit, prophetic ministry, intercession, and evangelism. XP Ministries/XPmedia is called to spreading the gospel through media.

Author Contact Information

U.S. Ministry Center
P.O. Box 1017
Maricopa, AZ 85139

Canada Ministry Center
3054 Springfield Road
Kelowna, B.C VIX 1A5

E-mail: info@XPmedia.com
www.xpministries.com
www.xpmedia.com
www.xpmissions.com
www.patriciaking.com

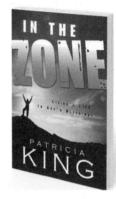

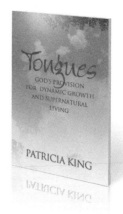

An Invitation to Spend Time with God

Sacred Time – Sacred Place, a Journal

This beautiful imitation leather journal has valuable tools to develop a rich devotional life. It includes practical guidelines to help you have a fruitful devotional time with Jesus, a plan to read the Bible in one year, and plenty of lined pages with a Bible Scripture at the bottom. Packaged in a gift box.

Unlock the Doors of Your Destiny!

Convergence–Heaven's Destiny Becoming Your Reality, by Patricia Bootsma. The fulfillment of prophetic words spoken over us depends on our response. Paul exhorted believers to "wage war" for personal prophecies. But how does one wage war for a prophetic word and then journey from promise to fulfillment? That question burned in Patricia's heart as she sought the Lord about how to walk in the things He promised her through prophecies. Walk beside her on her journey of discovery so the Lord can reveal to you the keys to unlock the doors of your destiny.

Additional copies of this book and other book titles
from Patricia King, XP Ministries and XP Publishing
are available at XPmedia.com

Wholesale prices for stores and ministries

In the U.S., please contact: usaresource@xpmedia.com.
In Canada, please contact:
resource@xpmedia.com.

XP Publishing books are also available to
wholesale and retail stores through
anchordistributors.com

www.XPpublishing.com

XP Ministries